Organizing music
in libraries

Organizing music in libraries

by Brian Redfern FLA

CLIVE BINGLEY  LONDON

FIRST PUBLISHED 1966 BY CLIVE BINGLEY LTD
16 PEMBRIDGE ROAD LONDON W11
SET IN LINOTYPE 10 ON 11 POINT TIMES ROMAN
AND PRINTED IN GREAT BRITAIN
BY THE CENTRAL PRESS (ABERDEEN) LTD

Contents

Preface

THIS BOOK IS INTENDED mainly for library students who intend to take professional examinations, but it is hoped that practising librarians may find something of value in its pages, while those who play and listen to music may possibly enjoy a glance at an unusual aspect of their art.

The title should really be prefaced by the phrase 'An introduction to . . .', as one day I would like to write at greater length on this fascinating subject and I am very conscious of the gaps in this book. I have not attempted, for example, to cover all the classification schemes and cataloguing codes, but have only discussed those I feel to be the most significant. Both the student and the librarian will find useful material in all the works mentioned. If this book is dedicated to anybody, it should be to those who have produced the schemes, codes and lists discussed in its pages and I hope it may stimulate others to a further study of them.

I am grateful to many who have helped either knowingly or unknowingly in creating this book, especially Derek Langridge and E T Bryant, who have both read the manuscript and contributed many ideas in conversations. Students past and present at the North-Western Polytechnic have all provoked thought on the subject, for lecturing is always a two-way process. Miss Evelyn Smith and Mrs Maureen Buckingham deserve special praise for typing the manuscript for me at great speed, and I am very grateful to my wife for her forbearance with my procrastinations and for her care in checking errors of style etc. With all this help, the faults remain mine.

Abbreviations used in the text are: BBC, British Broadcasting Corporation; BC, Bibliographic classification (Bliss); BCM, *British catalogue of music* classification; BNB, *British national bibliography;* DC, Decimal classification (Dewey); LC, Library of Congress classification. I should add that those parts reproduced directly from these classification schemes are copyright and may not be copied or reproduced without permission from the copyright owners.

Brian Redfern SENIOR LECTURER

NORTH-WESTERN POLYTECHNIC SCHOOL OF LIBRARIANSHIP

Glossary

Composite subject: a subject composed of two or more basic elements, *eg* 'piano concerto' is a composite subject of the two elements piano and concerto.

Expressive notation: one which reveals the structure of the subject as arranged by the classification.

Facet: a group of sub-divisions of a subject, all of which have a common feature, which only the members of that group possess and which gives its name to that group, *eg* a facet of music is 'instrument', all the sub-divisions in this group having the common characteristic of being the medium by which the music is produced by the player.

Focus: a sub-division within a facet, *eg* 'piano' is a focus within the facet 'instrument'.

Literature: books about music.

Music: scores.

Phase relationship: a relationship between two main classes of knowledge, *eg* music and religion.

Plate number: serial number given to each work by a music publisher and usually found at the foot of each page of the score.

Reader: a person who uses a library to consult or borrow any book, score, gramophone record or any other kind of material.

Score: a musical work in manuscript or printed form, generally used for works for two or more performers. A *full score* is a complete orchestral or conductor's score, containing all the parts, instrumental and/or vocal, fully set out. A *miniature score* is a pocket size reduction of a full score. A *vocal score* consists of the original vocal parts with a reduction for piano of the orchestral parts. A *piano score* is a reduction for piano of a work for orchestra.

CHAPTER ONE

Problems of organizing material

THERE ARE FOUR FACTORS which affect the organization of material in music and gramophone libraries. These are: money, time, people, material.

As far as this book is concerned the last two require the most attention, but the factors of money and time should not be neglected, for they affect the quantity and quality of any service.

MONEY

Most libraries depend on public funds for their money. This can be a useful limiting factor, by preventing the librarian who is too concerned with theory from letting his ideas control his practice. It can also kill good ideas. Before starting any catalogue of music two questions should be asked: 'How much is it going to cost?' and 'Is it worth it?'

In answering the first question, the cost of staff as well as the cost of equipment must be remembered. Sometimes the staff cost of cataloguing and classification is hidden in the total cost of all staff in an establishment, but, if possible, component staff costs should always be carefully estimated.

The answer to the second question depends on a very simple rule: *if the library will function properly without a catalogue, then one need not be provided.*

Working from this basic rule the librarian can decide what additional information he needs to provide above that given by the order of the material on the shelves. For example, if all enquiries are for scores by the name of the composer and the scores are arranged alphabetically by composer, there is little point in providing a catalogue arranged by form. The shelves give all the information needed.

In deciding what additional information to provide in the catalogue only general and frequent enquiries should be considered. Attempting to anticipate all possible types of enquiry only results in confusion and waste of money. A good catalogue is intended to be used frequently and to answer questions which occur regularly.

TIME

Catalogues are expensive items in terms of time. Not only does the initial compilation occupy a lot of staff output, but also the maintenance of, for example, authors' names, or correct subject terminology can consume more time than is sometimes realized. This problem is not confined to scientific libraries, as is sometimes suggested. At the same time most libraries, except those concerned with the preservation of material, have to remove records for material which has been lost or withdrawn. Therefore the basic rule cited above should be our point of commencement. From it an estimate can be made of the time likely to be involved in providing a catalogue of real value.

This question of time needs to be especially remembered if a decision has to be made whether to provide an additional catalogue. Many catalogues have been started with the best intention of giving an extra service, but after a short period they are found to be too costly in terms of time and abandoned. ' We never find time to keep it up to date ' is the excuse often made. It is much better not to provide a service than to offer it and then take it away.

PEOPLE

The second fundamental rule for all cataloguers is: *the reader is the most important person to consider.*

Before arranging the material, and the catalogues to it, a careful analysis must therefore be made of readers' needs. Only after this has been done and the material itself analyzed, can arrangement and cataloguing proceed.

The readers and the content of the material in the library are the factors which determine the best order to be selected from the many available. It is important to remember that, if all usual enquiries are to be met satisfactorily, the librarian may require certain information which he may use to help the reader, but which the latter never needs. A simple example of this is the accession number which is often provided on a catalogue entry. A more complex example is the name of the publisher, which to a good librarian can sometimes be a clue to the authority of the book.

Music librarians are faced with special problems in considering the needs of their readers, for there are many different ways in which music and music literature can be approached. Not all libraries will have all the most common types of readers, but we need to consider all classes here. The following is a list of main reader categories with examples of the approach each may make. It must be appreciated that individuals cannot be pigeon-holed in this way. One man in his time will play many parts. We are separating the parts.

1 *Musicologist or research worker*: His approach may well be simply by composer. His research having been done in reference books, he probably knows what he wants. However, he might find that an historical order provokes new ideas and needs.

2 *Instrumentalist*: This category of reader generally prefers material to be arranged by instrument. Form may also prove a useful arranging device.

3 *Music teacher*: Arrangement according to degree of difficulty might prove most serviceable here, though once again instrument could be an important factor.

4 *Groups of players, singers, etc*: Here an approach might depend on the number of people involved. It is interesting to note that *String music in print* (see ' Bibliography ' on page 77) arranges by the number of instruments.

5 *General readers and students*: The most difficult group to analyze. They may require many different approaches and find the one which the librarian selects unsatisfactory.

6 *Readers who borrow gramophone records*: This is a comparatively new group, whose main approach is probably by composer but a new factor here is the performing artist or orchestra. Records will be discussed in chapter six as a separate item.

It can be seen immediately from this list why so many national and university libraries arrange their material and catalogues by composer. It is the simplest arrangement and one which will probably suit most of their readers, who will be either musicologists or students. The latter are usually given lists by their lecturers and will therefore approach the shelves by name of composer in the case of music and by name of author when looking for literature.

MATERIAL
We have to consider finally the material which is to be arranged. Once we have analyzed this and seen what elements exist in the kinds of material a music library stocks, we can group these

elements together according to their degrees of likeness. These groups will provide the categories by which our material can be arranged.

A note of confusion can creep in here, which can be avoided best by adopting the simple technical terms proposed by Dr Ranganathan. This eminent Indian librarian is owed a debt of gratitude for the simplicity of his approach to problems in classification, and his work will be discussed at several points throughout this book. Definitions of these terms will be found in the glossary on page 8.

To decide what order we are going to use in arranging a library, we must examine a quantity of the material and break each title down into elements. This examination of the material should continue until no new *facets* are obviously being revealed. This could be after the examination of as many as two hundred titles. It is not proposed to analyze as many titles as that here, but only to use sufficient titles to demonstrate the method.

The first five titles will help the student to understand the technique. After that he should attempt to analyze the remaining titles himself before checking his answers against those given below.

1 A companion to Mozart's piano concertos. **Foci:** Mozart / piano / concertos / literature.

2 The Oxford school harmony course. **Foci:** schools / harmony / literature.

3 The sonata [form] in the classic era. **Foci:** sonata form / classic era / literature.

4 Prokofiev—symphony no 6—miniature score. **Foci:** Prokofiev / symphony / orchestra / score.

5 Bach—sonata no 2—for solo violin. **Foci:** Bach / sonata / solo / violin / score.

It is immediately obvious that certain foci belong to the same facet *eg Mozart, Prokofiev, Bach;* whereas the focus *solo,* while not belonging to the same group as any other focus so far isolated, may well suggest the facet to which it ultimately belongs if its nature is considered.

To simplify matters students will find it convenient to use a separate slip of paper or card for each facet and to list the appropriate foci on each slip as they occur in the titles below. It should be emphasized that these titles have been selected to arrive at a quick analysis. In normal circumstances with titles selected at random all the facets would not be so quickly revealed. The remaining titles are:

6 The songs of Hugo Wolf—study.

7 Mozart's clarinet quintet—score and parts.

8 The symphonies of Sibelius—a study.

9 Bartok's piano concertos—study scores.
10 Haydn's string quartets—study scores.
11 Vaughan Williams' romance for viola and piano—score.
12 Haydn's mass in time of war—full score.
13 Mozart's operas—study.
14 Strict tempo dance arrangements.
15 Film music of the thirties—arranged for piano.
16 A selection of folk songs arranged for four part choir.
17 Modes for folk singers.
18 Bach's use of counterpoint in his fugues.
19 A thematic catalogue of Beethoven's works.
20 A dictionary of church music.
21 The influence of architecture on the music of Gabrieli.
22 Teach yourself to compose music.
23 Orchestration in Italian operas.
24 Musical aesthetics.
25 The effect of climate on Irish pipes.
26 The physics of music.

Some of these titles are easy to analyze but others do present difficulties. We may have to abandon initial ideas not only in our analysis, but also in our grouping into categories. The suggested analysis is:

 6 Songs/voice/Wolf/literature.
 7 Mozart/clarinet/quintet/ensemble/score.
 8 Symphonies/Sibelius/literature.
 9 Bartok/piano/concerto/score.
10 Haydn/strings/quartets/ensembles/scores.
11 Vaughan Williams/viola/piano/duo/score.
12 Haydn/mass/score.
13 Mozart/operas/literature.
14 Tempo/dance/arrangements.
15 Films/thirties/arrangements/piano/score.
16 Folk music/songs/arrangements/four parts/choir/score.
17 Modes/folk music/voices/literature.
18 Bach/counterpoint/fugue/literature.
19 Catalogue/themes/Beethoven/literature.
20 Dictionary/church/literature.
21 Architecture/Gabrieli/ literature.
22 Composition/literature.
23 Orchestration/Italy/operas/literature.
24 Aesthetics/literature.
25 Climate/Irish/pipes/literature.
26 Physics/literature.

The resulting categories are:

facet one	facet two	facet three
literature	composition	Italy
scores	orchestration	Irish

facet four	facet five	facet six
architecture	classic era	catalogues
climate	thirties	dictionaries

facet seven	facet eight	facet nine
harmony	schools	solo
tempo	dance	quintet
modes	films	duo
counterpoint	folk music	quartet
themes	church	four part

facet ten	facet eleven	facet twelve
concertos	piano	Mozart
symphonies	viola	Prokofiev
sonatas	voice	Bach
songs	orchestra	Sibelius
masses	clarinet	Bartok
operas	ensemble	Haydn
	strings	Vaughan
	viola	Williams
	choir	Beethoven
	pipes	Gabrieli

facet thirteen	facet fourteen	
sonata form	aesthetics	
fugues	physics	(arrangements)

One point is immediately apparent from this analysis. The music librarian has to contend not only with the literature on the subject, but also with the raw material itself. Ideally it would be best to have the literature dealing with the music arranged in the same place as the scores of that music, but if the basic nature of books and scores is considered it will be realized that this presents difficulties of a practical kind owing to the format of scores. A further point is that the music is presented in many different formats such as sheet music (example no 11) full score (no 12) score and parts (no 7) and miniature score (no 4). This prevents these formats from being satisfactorily arranged in one sequence. Full and miniature scores will contain the same music, the latter often being a photographic reduction of the former, but to place them side by side on the same shelf would mean valuable space being wasted and the miniature score's disappearance behind the larger volume. Therefore, before we begin to consider the essential characteristics of the material, we have to recognize that for practical purposes it is better to separate the scores from the literature and to arrange the scores according to format.

It is possible as a result of this decision that some of the facets our examination has revealed may not belong to both literature and music. This is confirmed by checking the items which revealed a particular facet. For example *facet seven,* which groups together the *elements* a composer may use in composing music, has foci appearing in items 2, 14, 17, 18, 19. All these items are literature and in fact it is extremely unlikely that music would be sought under such terms as 'harmony', 'counterpoint' and 'tempo'. Even collections of examples of such elements will probably be better classified with the literature, for it is with the study of the subject that they really belong.

Other facets which appear in the literature only are *two (questions of technique), four (other subjects outside music), six (forms of presentation)* and *fourteen (theory of music).* There may be others which we shall decide are best used only in connection with the literature, but those so far considered are probably limited to it.

First it is necessary to settle which facets are important in any arrangement of the music. These are *nine (size of ensemble), ten (musical form), eleven (instrument)* and *twelve (composer).* These are equally important in the arrangement of the literature.

This leaves the following:

Facet three: This can be called a geographical or space facet. It must be considered as a possible method of arrangement and will certainly need to be expressed in many divisions of the literature, where studies of the music of geographical areas abound. It is doubtful whether the music needs to be arranged by this space facet, however, as this is not a primary retrieval term for music except in special cases such as folk music or Italian opera, where this represents a style of composition rather than a geographical entity.

Facet five: This provides the historical approach and could be very important for the musicologist, as we have seen. But, once again, while it will need to be expressed in arranging literature where there are many historical studies, it is doubtful whether in general it will be needed for music.

Facet eight: This is an interesting group. It is difficult to find a satisfactory name for it, as these foci all represent purposes for which music has been written. The *British catalogue of music*

(BCM) classification uses the term 'musical character', which seems as satisfactory as any. It could be used in arranging both literature and scores, although as far as the latter is concerned some foci will be more important than others. It would seem useful to show what music has been composed for schools, for example, but perhaps not so necessary to separate music for the dance.

Facet thirteen: This is very close to *musical form* and would appear to be important in both literature and music. In relation to *musical form* it can be said that those foci isolated in *ten* represent the larger forms, while those in *thirteen* are the smaller forms. Sonata form may be used in concertos, symphonies, masses and operas as well as in sonatas. Some forms, such as rondo form, may appear in either facet. It is possible that some of the smaller forms will not need expression in arranging scores. Examples are first movement or sonata form, binary and ternary forms.

To sum up, the facets to be considered in arranging the literature are: *composers, instruments, forms, techniques, elements, musical character, size of ensemble, theory, period* or *history, space* or *geographical area, form of presentation, other subjects influencing music*. This last is really part of what is called a *phase relationship* and is better so defined.

These facets can be divided into two groups. Some of them are very general in their nature and because we tend to approach subjects in a general way first we would expect them to appear first in any arrangement. These are *theory, phase relationship, history, techniques, form of presentation, geographical area*. The others are more specific and are *composers, instruments, forms, elements, musical character, size of ensemble*. The order of facets in the second group will vary from library to library and depend on the kind of information the readers require. It is not possible to say which of the possible permutations is best. The choice must depend on a given situation. In a library where study of the composer is the primary concern we would expect to find literature arranged first by the composer facet, followed possibly by form and then by instrument, but in another situation the order might very well be *form—instrument—composer*. This would mean that in a library arranged under the first order the books would appear on the shelves as follows: general studies—composers—forms—instruments; and in the second library: general studies—forms—instruments—composers.

Unfortunately books do not deal with single subjects such as 'Mozart', or 'Pianos' and 'concertos', but are much more likely to deal with 'Mozart's piano concertos'. Any arrangement must allow for this and there are two ways of providing for these com-

16

posite subjects. The traditional method is to be found in such schemes as the Library of Congress classification, which attempts to enumerate all the possible composite subjects. The modern method is found in BCM classification, which provides the foci within the facets and rules on combining these foci to form composite subjects.

Thus for the first library above the traditional method would produce this sample order:

A1	Beethoven	
A2	Haydn	
A3	Mozart	
A3·1		Concertos
A3·11		Piano
A3·2		Symphonies
B1	Fugues	
B2	Suites	
B3	Concertos	
B3·1		Piano
c1	Violin	
c2	Cello	
c3	Piano	

Thus the book on Mozart's piano concertos would go at A3·11 and not at B3·1, because it was decided that in this particular library composer was the most important aspect and because a fundamental rule of all classification is that an item must be placed in the most specific head that will contain it. Nevertheless the traditional method does result occasionally in confusion and cross classification if care is not exercised.

The modern method would provide the facets in a given order, listing the foci under each facet:

Composers
1 Beethoven
2 Haydn
3 Mozart
Forms
1 Concertos
2 Symphonies
3 Fugues
Instruments
1 Piano
2 Cellos
3 Violas

The scheme would provide clear instructions on the order of combination of terms from these facets. In this example the com-

17

bination order would be composers/forms/instruments. Thus the book must be analyzed into Mozart/piano/concertos. These foci are then placed in their correct combination order Composer= Mozart/Form=concertos/Instrument=piano. The number for each focus is then taken from its appropriate facet and combined in order to give the final number for the book 311.

The advantage of the newer method is apparent immediately we have to classify a book on a composite subject which has not been catered for by the traditional scheme. For example, until recently Haydn was not considered as a composer of operas, but now there is great interest in this side of his activity. Because of the earlier neglect our traditional scheme would probably not have specified

Haydn operas

and somehow a place would have to be made. The modern or faceted scheme would have provided

Composers
Haydn
Form
Operas

Therefore the composite subject can easily be formed by combining the two numbers in the correct order.

The main facets to be considered in the arrangement of music scores are *composers, instruments, forms, size of ensemble*. Other facets which may need to be considered are *character, space, time*. The same principles will apply here as in the arrangement of musical literature and the two methods of classification will be found in use in arranging scores.

Two further points need to be considered, however, in relation to the scores. The first is the frequency with which arrangements are met in music. It is one of the major problems of cataloguing music, but is it a problem in placing the material on the shelves? Here once again the answer must depend on the kind of library. A public library where most readers will want music for a particular instrument need not consider this problem. The flautist wants music for the flute, whether originally scored or arranged for his instrument. A learned society's library on the other hand might well have to take account of arrangements and specify them under a composer, for example, further indicating the original instrumentation.

The second point is the very obvious division which needs to be made, in dealing with scores, between vocal and instrumental music. It would seem logical to extend this division to the literature. It is generally accepted that mixed vocal/instrumental scores are placed with the vocal group.

In this chapter the main concern has been to analyze the basic problems of organizing material, by examining the kinds of approaches that readers make in music libraries and reducing the contents of books and scores to their basic elements. It can be seen that readers' needs are matched by these elements and therefore the problems can be solved very simply by individual librarians by making their primary arrangement equal the primary need of their readers. Unfortunately not all librarians have readers whose needs fall into one category. Therefore having decided on an order for the material on the shelves most suited to the needs of the majority of their readers, they must help others by supplementing that order by means of catalogues. Thus if an order for the shelves is used which gives priority to the instrument, the reader interested in music by a particular composer can be helped by means of a composer catalogue.

In attempting to help the reader interested in particular subjects within music such as harmony, acoustics, opera and film music to find his material, the librarian has a variety of methods to consider. These will be discussed together with other specifically cataloguing problems in chapters four and five.

We conclude this chapter with a tabulated list of the facets revealed in music. This will be found useful in the following chapters where the major schemes are examined.

FACETS IN MUSIC
1 Facets in literature and music
    1 Composers
    2 Instruments
    3 Size of ensemble
    4 Forms
       a Major (*eg* concertos)
       b Minor (*eg* binary)
2 Facets in literature and possibly in music
    5 Musical character
    6 Space (*ie* country etc)
    7 Time (*ie* baroque etc)
3 Facets in literature and unlikely in music
    8 Elements (*ie* harmony etc)
    9 Techniques (*ie* orchestration etc)
    10 Theory (*ie* appreciation etc)
    11 Forms of presentation (*ie* catalogues)
    12 Phase relationship (*ie* music interrelated with other subjects)

CHAPTER TWO

The BCM classification

THE BCM FIRST APPEARED in 1957 and its publication was one of the most important events in the history of music publishing. It is not necessary to discuss its bibliographical importance here, as we are concerned only with its possibilities as a classification scheme. It is not irrelevant to mention that music publishers, booksellers and continental as well as British librarians have all been known to pay tribute to the simplicity with which it can be used.

The scheme was designed principally by E J Coates, at that time on the staff of BNB, in close consultation with members of the United Kingdom branch of the International Association of Music Libraries. It is therefore an interesting example of collaboration between a classification specialist and people fully acquainted with the problems of attempting to organize the subject literature in libraries. It is important in the history of classification as the first *printed* fully faceted scheme published in Great Britain. It is based, therefore, on the principles of classification developed by Dr Ranganathan.

The literature of music is quite clearly separated from scores, and whenever possible the same notation is used for parallel subjects:

AS Books on the violin

s Scores for violin

Violin, the common factor here, is represented by s. The schedules provide places and notation for foci in various facets of music. The user of the scheme expresses the composite subjects in books and scores by combining the notational elements for the appropriate foci to produce a composite number. Thus:

WT=horn
E =sonata
Sonata for horn=WTE.

Following the principles considered in chapter one, we would expect a rule of procedure to be provided for number building. The rule for this scheme can probably be understood if an outline of the structure is given:

Outline tables

A—BZ LITERATURE OF MUSIC

A	General works
A(B)—A(WT)	Common subdivisions
A(X)	History of music
A(Y)	Music in particular localities
A(Z)	Music in relation to other subjects
A/AM	Theory
A/CY	Technique
A/FY	Musical character
A/LZ	Elements
A/S	Forms (*ie* binary etc)
AB	Vocal music
AL	Instrumental music
B	Biographies and studies of composers
BZ	Non-European music

C—Z MUSIC—SCORES

CB	Vocal music
L	Instrumental music
Z	Non-European music

At the beginning of the section for SCORES under C an arrangement is provided for educational material consisting primarily of exercises not limited to a particular instrument, collected works of individual composers and collections of illustrative music. All of these symbols can be applied to symbols drawn from the vocal and instrumental classes. This will be demonstrated in examining the treatment of vocal music. Some examples of the type of material classed at the beginning of class C follow:—

C/AC	Tutors
C/AZ	Collections from individual composers
C/G—C/L	Collections to illustrate music of a particular character
C/G	Folk music
C/H	Dance music
C/JR	Film music
C/L	Religious music

| c/LZ | Collections illustrating the various elements of music |
| c/s | Collections illustrating the various forms |

A slightly more detailed outline of the arrangement under class
L INSTRUMENTAL MUSIC follows:

M	Orchestral music
MP	Solo instrument and orchestra
MT	Jazz
N	Chamber music
PW	Keyboard instruments
RW	String instruments
RX	Bowed
T	Plucked
U	Wind instruments

It can be seen from this that the arrangement is from large to small groups and that the instruments are arranged according to the method by which they are played. It is also apparent that the notation is not expressive.

Several auxiliary tables are provided. The first is the most important as it includes sub-arrangements for use under instruments and instrumental groups. This enables such facets as *form* and *size* to be expressed simply. Certain parts of this table can be applied to orchestral and chamber music. Other tables are special subdivisions for keyboard instruments, ethnic or locality subdivisions (*space* facet) and chronological reference points (*time* facet).

There are two indexes, the first being to the table of ethnic or locality subdivisions and the second a general subject index to the main tables. This index must never be used as a substitute for the tables in classifying. It is only an index to the elements which appear in the schedules and it does not include any composite subjects.

An examination of the outline table will show that the general or diffuse concepts in music come first (theory, technique) while the more concrete come last (composers, instruments). The rule for forming composite numbers is simply: *Arrange elements of a title in reverse schedule order.*

Apply this to the example:
  sonata for horn
Schedule order:
  E   sonata
  WT   horn
Reverse schedule order:
  horn/sonata
  WTE

Therefore the order in expressing a composite subject is from the concrete to the diffuse, or from a thing to an idea.

Schedules:

    idea / diffuse / general—concrete / thing
    sonata   horn

Composite subject in a score or book:

    concrete / thing—idea / diffuse / general
    horn   sonata

In discussing order in chapter one a sample schedule was built up (page 17) in which the schedule order was the same as the order of the elements in a composite subject. The principle is exactly the same in the BCM scheme. All that has been done is to reverse the schedule order because usually it has been found that readers approach knowledge from the general to the particular. A simple example of this is the method of any study which usually works from the general to the particular.

Students sometimes find difficulty in understanding this procedure, but anyone using this scheme need not worry, for the introduction explains the method and there are tables giving the main facets for both scores and literature, in the order in which each may contribute elements to the composite subjects.

For scores and parts:

EXECUTANT	FORM OF COMPOSITION	CHARACTER
piano	suite	Christmas

The EXECUTANT facet has the following sub-facets, expressed in this order:

1 *Vocal music*

SIZE OR COMPLEXITY	TYPE	ACCOMPANIMENT
duets	baritone	piano

2 *Instrumental music*

TYPE	SIZE	ACCOMPANIMENT	ORIGINAL EXECUTANT
flute	solo	none	oboe

For musical literature

COMPOSER	EXECUTANT	FORM	ELEMENTS	CHARACTER
Bach	organ	fugue	counterpoint	

TECHNIQUE	COMMON SUBDIVISION
sight reading	

The title chosen here is imaginary and unlikely, but it shows the use of these tables. With any title it is simply a matter of asking a number of questions in the correct order. Thus:

Sight reading Bach's counterpoint in his fugues for organ.

QUESTION		ANSWER	
1	Who is the *composer*?	1	Bach
2	What or who is the *executant*?	2	Organ
3	What is the *form*?	3	Fugue
4	What is the *element*?	4	Counterpoint
5	What is the *musical character*?	5	—
6	What is the *technique*?	6	Sight reading
7	What is the *common-subdivision*?	7	—

Having asked the questions, the classifier must then consult the schedules with the answers to build the correct number. The questions were asked in reverse schedule order, therefore the notational elements must combine in that way.

Terms in schedule order with notation:

6	Sight reading	A/EAG
4	Counterpoint	A/RM
3	Fugue	A/Y
2	Organ	AR
1	Bach	BBC

Instructions under B explain that, in adding symbols to a biography number, the initial A is retained when adding symbols from AB—AY, but those drawn from A(A)—A/Z drop the initial A. Therefore taking the notational element for each answer in reverse schedule order, *ie* the order in which the questions were asked, gives the composite symbol:

BBCAR/Y/RM/EAG

This is a very long number, which draws attention to a criticism frequently made, namely, that the symbols in the *British catalogue of music* are too long. There are several points to make here:

1 This was an imaginary title, deliberately designed to introduce as many facets as possible. No other scheme could express all these elements.

2 The scheme is used as the basis of arrangement of a national bibliography. It is used as the filing medium in the main part of the bibliography and as a link between that part and the alphabetical index. Its length and accuracy enables an item to be placed very precisely and it also ensures that all concepts will be expressed in the index by isolating them in analysis.

3 Because this is a faceted scheme the classifier using the scheme in a library can modify it easily to suit his own purpose. The composite symbols are not supplied by the scheme, but constructed by the classifier. He need only use that part of the composite symbol

co-extensive with the needs of his readers. In a given library situation this might be :

BBC AR/Y *Bach's organ fugues.*

For indexing purposes he would be advised to work out the complete number, but index to the final limited symbol those terms expressed by elements beyond that part of the symbol selected :

Sight reading : Counterpoint : Fugues : Organ : Bach BBC AR/Y
and
Counterpoint : Fugues : Organ : Bach BBC AR/Y

This would ensure that the reader interested in those concepts would not be neglected.

Reference was made above to the use made in the bibliography of the classification as a filing medium. A feature here is the very broad base achieved by use of three sets of symbols (A)—(Z), /A—/Z and A—Z. The arranging or filing order of these symbols is always : ( )/A—Z.

The advantage of this is that the basic terms are expressed by very simple numbers. As the notation makes no attempt to express the relationship between subjects, it is easy to accommodate new subjects whenever they may be required. This is demonstrated from PW KEYBOARD INSTRUMENTS :

Q	Piano
QR	Harpsichord
QS	Spinet
QSQ	Virginals
QT	Glockenspiel (keyed)
QY	Celeste

As the notation does not express relationship, a new instrument in this family can be accommodated at any convenient point, due regard being made to any possible clash with existing symbols. QP is used in auxiliary table 2 for *piano solos,* but QZ has not been used and by adopting that symbol a whole possible range of extensions is opened for any future instruments in the family. With an expressive notation attempting to show relationships this would not be such a simple exercise.

The brevity of the notation in comparison with the Decimal and Library of Congress classifications is shown by the following three common examples. This seems a fairer method than by selection of esoteric titles which some critics have used :

	BCM	DC	LC
Sonata for oboe	VTE	788·7	M67
Concerto for clarinet and orchestra	MPVVF	785·686204	M1024
Missa solemnis—full score	EMDG	783·2254	M2010

These three examples are typical of the majority of scores with which a classifier has to contend. In all three the BCM notation is no more difficult than that of either DC or LC. Yet in each case all the concepts are expressed by BCM, but in the first, for example, LC does not express *sonata* while in DC all that can be expressed is *double reed instrument*.

One feature in which the BCM scheme does seem excessively detailed is in the lengths to which the notation is taken to express the original executant in an arrangement. A simple example is:
Piano arrangement of Bizet's *Carmen*.

Q   Piano
QP   Solo (from auxiliary table 2)
K/   Arrangements (from auxiliary table 1)
CC   Opera

giving QPK/CC.

This means that all arrangements for solo piano from opera file together and all arrangements from pieces for, say, clarinet come together; but is the pianist really interested in the original scoring to the extent that he requires to have all arrangements of marches from films classed together at QPK/MGM/JR?

MGM   Marches
M   Orchestral music
GM   Marches (from auxiliary table 1)
C/JR   Film music (the C is dropped in composite symbols).

It would seem sufficient to separate arrangements from works originally scored for the particular instrument or combination as LC does. It should be pointed out that the introduction to BCM does allow that opinions on this point will differ, and suggests the expression of instrumental arrangements of vocal works and of reductions of works for solo instrument and orchestra for the same instrument with piano accompaniment.

Combinations of instruments are very easily indicated in BCM. Instructions are to be found under N CHAMBER MUSIC. Some examples follow:
Sonata for viola and piano. (Entry is made under the later symbol where instruments belong to different families.)

Viola SQ
Piano P (auxiliary table 1)
Sonatas E
SQPE

Suite for violin and cello. (Entry is made under the earlier symbol when instruments belong to the same family.)

S   Violin
SR   Cello

G   Suites

SSRG

String quartet. (Combinations of more than two limited to one family are entered under the family.)

RX   Bowed string instruments

NS   Quartets

RXNS

Piano trio. (Special symbols are provided under N for mixed family ensembles of more than two instruments.)

NX   String and keyboard ensembles

NT   Trios

NXNT

Vocal music is dealt with in basically the same way as instrumental music. An outline of that section of the schedules gives:

CB   Vocal music

CC   Opera

D   Choral music

DC   Oratorios, cantatas, masses

DW   Songs

E   Choral works with an accompaniment other than keyboard instrument

EZ   Unaccompanied choral works

F-HY Choral works. Special voices

F   Female

FL   Soprano

J   Unison choral works

JN   Single voices in combination

K   Vocal solos

Some examples follow to demonstrate this part in use:

Messiah—vocal score. Class D is used for vocal scores with keyboard accompaniment.

DD   Oratorios

Messiah—full score. Full scores go under E, the accompaniment being shown by the appropriate symbol from the instrumental section. In the case of orchestral accompaniment this is actually provided in the schedules EM.

DD   Oratorios

EMDD

Christmas carols for unaccompanied male voices

C/LF Christmas

DP   Carols

EZ   Unaccompanied choral works

G   Male voices

GEZDP/LF (*Note*: in adding symbols from C/ the C is dropped.)

Examples of composite numbers for single voices are given in the schedules. It is impossible to give examples covering every combination, but those given in this chapter should demonstrate the great flexibility of this scheme.

The literature of the subject is handled in the same way, except that the composer facet comes first in any composite symbol where appropriate. This can be clearly seen in the imaginary Bach example given earlier (page 23).

The ethnic/locality subdivisions in auxiliary table 6 are very full for Commonwealth countries and the United States, but not developed at all for other countries. This seems a pity in the case of countries such as Austria and Italy with a great musical tradition. Surely Vienna and Salzburg are met more frequently in music literature than, say, Norfolk or Nebraska. It does mean that countries, other than the United States and those of the Commonwealth in the Western European tradition, would have to alter this part of the scheme to suit their own needs. Countries in the non-European tradition are treated more fully at BZ. Symbols taken from table 6 are introduced by (Y . . .). Thus *Church music in Great Britain* would be A/LD (YC) where A/LD is CHURCH MUSIC and C is BRITISH from table 6. They can be added directly to /AY to indicate a collection of music relating to a particular country. It is not proposed to discuss table 7 (chronological reference points) as it seems unlikely that any library would use it and it is not an essential part of the scheme.

Greater attention has been given to this scheme than to any others described below because it is the first major scheme to be produced by British librarians for music and it is an intrinsic part of the National Bibliography of music. Any reader who wishes to study it further can do so by taking any issue of the *British catalogue of music* and comparing his composite numbers for any title with those provided by the bibliography. It is important to work from the facet orders provided by the introduction to the scheme and set out on page 23 of the present book, as indeed it is in checking any of the examples given above.

It is always possible to criticize any work adversely and one or two such comments follow. In reading them it should be remembered that, in the present writer's opinion, this scheme is the finest classification of music in print. It arranges the facets of music in an order which is convenient to the majority of readers of most libraries, and for expressing composite subjects it provides a systematic approach which places both books and scores under the basic terms which are likely to be used by the majority of readers. Most readers wanting a book on Mozart's piano concertos will surely have the composer primarily in mind and most instrumentalists wanting music will surely want the music for their instrument in the same place, not separated under form or composer. Both needs are met by the BCM scheme. Obviously some libraries will require a different arrangement, however, and an interesting view on this is provided by Maurice B Line in the article listed in the bibliography on page 77.

JAZZ is placed at AMT between LIGHT ORCHESTRAL MUSIC and CHAMBER MUSIC. The form *jazz* for a particular instrument can be expressed by HX from auxiliary table 1. Better treatment would be to place it at BX, which has not been used and comes conveniently between music of the European tradition and the non-European tradition at BZ. This seems a very suitable place for a developed classification of jazz to appear. This idea was suggested to me by my colleague Derek Langridge.

It would be interesting to know why A/D(M) was used for collective biography of composers. It seems more logical for this to appear at B before the biographies of individual composers. Presumably such omissions can be easily rectified, but there are some curious gaps in the alphabetical list of composers at B. It is perhaps justifiable to specify some rather obscure English composers, but it seems odd to include Anton Diabelli and not Bohuslav Martinu, Ludwig Spohr, Johann Hummel and Karl von Dittersdorf.

It may seem unfortunate that vocal and full scores of such works as *Messiah* are separated at D and EM, but this is a convenient arrangement for the shelves as the format of each is so different from that of the other and in the bibliography they are brought together under the composer in the index.

CHAPTER THREE

Treatment of music
in some general
schemes of classification

IT IS NOT POSSIBLE in a book of this length to deal with the general schemes' treatment of music to quite the same extent as with the organization of material according to BCM. Instead, a brief general survey of each will be given.

LIBRARY OF CONGRESS

This is a very important classification of music. It is not so modern in construction as BCM but it is intended for use in large libraries and was developed out of the experience gained in organizing one of the largest and finest collections of music in the world. It is, therefore, an extremely practical scheme and any adverse criticism must be tempered by the knowledge that the Library of Congress does provide a fine service to musicians and scholars throughout the world.

It is a part (class M) of the complete Library of Congress classification, which has been constructed empirically since the beginning of this century. There is much to be said for the method used, which was to base the classification on a convenient arrangement of the books in the collection. Class M was published in 1904 and, like all the other main classes in the scheme, is complete in itself. LC is therefore a number of special subject schemes grouped together to form a specialist classification. This has the obvious advantage for a special library that individual parts can be purchased very cheaply. The cost of class M in Great Britain is still less than £1.

In the introduction, O G Sonneck, chief of the music division in 1904, stated that the scheme was based somewhat on the form of classified catalogue used by music publishers in arranging scores, and therefore appears somewhat different from the style favoured by librarians. This is really only a minor difference. It certainly does not prevent use of the scheme in libraries.

The schedules are divided into three main groups:

M   MUSIC
ML   MUSIC LITERATURE
MT   MUSIC INSTRUCTION AND STUDY

There is a combined relative index to all three sections at the back. It is important to realize that the schedules are constantly being revised in the light of experience. The tables are frequently reprinted and amendments, with their own index, are listed at the back of the volume after the general index. The amendments, which between each reprint are also listed in LC *Classification—additions and changes,* are not so drastic as to necessitate considerable reorganization and are often helpful solutions to current problems.

A list of definitions appears at the beginning of M. These should be read carefully as a number of terms are used in the scheme in a special way.

String instruments are defined as string instruments with a bow. Compare BCM where this group is subdivided into *bowed* and *plucked.* For the latter, LC uses *Plectral instruments.*

Early music is used for music published or manuscript before 1800, but in the class catalogue it means music composed before 1800.

It follows that in the schedules, the period division for published works depends on the date of publication, not of composition. It is interesting to note that in the preface to a revised edition issued in 1917, Sonneck felt that a completely separate arrangement for early music would have been better, since it does involve special problems such as the precise difference between vocal and instrumental music and between chamber and orchestral music.

The order in MUSIC (class M) is:

M1—M4 Collections with special places for *Monuments of music* (*ie* Denkmäler) and collected editions of individual composers with special recognition of the significance of the Breitkopf and Härtel *Gesamtausgaben.*

M5—M1459 Instrumental music—subdivided by *size* divided by *instrument.* Orchestral music is arranged at M1000—M1360.

M1490 Music (instrumental or vocal), printed or manuscript, before 1700 and preferred here, arranged by composers instead of assigned to special classes.

M1495—M2197 Vocal music—subdivided secular (M1497—M1998) and sacred (M1999—M2199).

31

Under instrumental music, as has been stated, the basic division is by size. The instruments under solo are arranged in the order: keyboard—string—wind—plectral—percussion. Within each instrumental group the order, where appropriate, is the same as full score order (*eg* flute—oboe—clarinet etc). Piano and organ are subdivided by form:

M20—39 Piano music
M23 Piano sonatas

Other instruments are divided into: miscellaneous collections; original compositions; arrangement.

Under some instruments (*eg* violin) a place is provided for *simplified editions,* but not under other instruments (*eg* flute). It would be interesting to know how the choice was made. It is difficult to believe that the Library of Congress has no simplified editions for clarinet. Arrangements are entered under the instrument for which the piece has been arranged.

Duos involving a piano are all entered under piano. This means that Brahms' *Sonatas for clarinet and piano* will be entered at M250 under duos for piano and clarinet and not at M72 under clarinet, as might be expected by most clarinet players.

Orchestral music is subdivided first by type of orchestra and then by form:

M1000—M1075 Symphony orchestra
M1001 Symphonies
M1004 Overtures, including opera overtures if detached (no specific place provided for those by BCM).
M1005—M1041 Concertos—divided by solo instrument.
M1100—M1160 String orchestra.

It is apparent from this that the order of applying facets in placing a composite score is: size of instrumental group/instrument/original composition or arrangement/form (for some instruments only).

Secular vocal music is arranged similarly by the size of the group, although while instrumental music proceeds from solo to orchestra, this starts with operas and finishes at solo songs:

M1500—M1529 Dramatic music
M1500 Operas—full scores
M1502 Vocal scores—unaccompanied
M1503 Vocal scores—piano accompaniment
M1530—M1546 Choral music—secular cantatas etc. Arranged—mixed, men's, women's, children's voices.
M1547—M1610 Choruses and part-songs, not originally intended for orchestra accompaniment as at M1530—M1546. Arranged—as M1530—M1546.

M1611—M1998 Songs, with a very detailed arrangement at the end of national songs arranged by country.

Sacred vocal music is arranged differently. Form is used as the basic characteristic:

M2000—M2007 Oratorios
M2010—M2017 Masses
M2018—M2036 Cantatas etc.

Under M2079 (chorus, anthems, part-songs) there is a very full arrangement for settings of special texts in Latin and in English.

At M2147—M2188 very full treatment is available for liturgies. This is for music only. The texts go in class B (religion).

The method of working, therefore, in classifying a vocal music score would be: secular or sacred (*ie* musical character) /form (in which size is implied by the order) /kind of voice (in most cases) /accompaniment.

MUSIC LITERATURE (ML) is arranged so that, as would be expected, general works come first, with librettos at ML48—ML54. History and criticism forms a very large class (ML159—ML3795). General histories come first, arranged by period, then the history of music in individual countries which are subdivided by use of a ' period table ' at ML197.

Biography of individual composers is placed at ML410. This would also include criticism, although analytical guides appear at MT90—MT150. There is an exceptionally detailed subdivision provided for Wagner, which it is claimed can be adapted for other exceptional composers. It would not be easy to adapt, however, and it would seem more sensible to make a special arrangement for each composer when required, although, as the scheme suggests, subdivision to any great detail under composers is probably best avoided.

There follows a somewhat haphazard and incomplete grouping of the two facets analyzed in chapter one as *elements* (rhythm, melody etc) and *techniques* (instrumentation) with *forms* (general) in the middle:

ML446 Counterpoint
ML448 Forms (general)
ML457 Conducting

There is no indication on how a book on the problems of conducting counterpoint should be classed; presumably, as the scheme goes from general to specific, under ML457. This is dealt with later (see page 34).

The *instrument* facet comes next, arranged in the same order as in M, followed by sections for chamber and orchestral music. Both these categories of music and the individual instruments are sub-divided by period and country. Books on vocal music follow, arranged similarly to the scores in M with country and period divisions where appropriate. Next ML has a grouping by country of books on national music (ML3545—ML3775), where a careful distinction must be made between this and the history of music in general in a particular country (ML200).

The final main division in ML is:

ML3800—ML3920 Philosophy and physics of music.

Here go all the books on such subjects as acoustics, physiology, aesthetics and ethics when they are related to music. This type of subject would usually be better placed in the general works section at the beginning of ML, but it may have been placed here because it is obviously closely linked to MT.

MUSICAL INSTRUCTION (MT) is a quite useful separation of books concerned with the teaching of different techniques in music, and particularly those devoted to individual instruments and the voice. The instruments are arranged in the same order as they are at M with subdivision under each instrument for: general observations; systems and methods; studies and exercises—general, orchestral, self-instructors.

At MT90 (analytical guides) there is a special arrangement for Wagner again. A note at MT90 explains that this symbol is used for books on how to listen and how to understand certain musical compositions. The more general studies will be placed at ML410. It is always possible to ignore MT90 and use ML410 for all books on a composer.

It is not easy to see the basic arrangement of either ML or MT in such a way that a book dealing with a composite subject can be classified with certainty. In fact it would probably be unfair to work out a facet order for composite subjects on the basis of the scheme. It would be safer, however, for a classifier, working in a library and using this scheme, to compile his own facet order and apply it in all cases in order to achieve uniformity in placing books. To do this he would need to employ the techniques outlined in chapter one.

As it stands, the scheme is too detailed for most libraries, but the compilers give full permission in the preface to the revised edition (1917) for any convenient modification to be carried out. There is always the danger of cross classification in schemes of the traditional type such as this, and some contraction of the schedules might reduce this risk. It is probable, too, that modern composers have written for combinations not covered in the LC schedules.

Jazz originated in the United States, but was of no special significance when the scheme appeared, nor even by 1917. It has had to be inserted since then and will be found only in the 'additions' at the back, where it is placed, under ML3551 United States, in the broad division national music, at ML3561. It has some odd companions, such as (also at 3561) A history of campaign songs, and ML3562 Festivals of civic patriotism.

This illustrates very clearly the difficulties of coping with new subjects in an enumerative scheme such as LC.

THE BLISS BIBLIOGRAPHIC CLASSIFICATION

It is hard to reconcile the lifetime spent by Henry Evelyn Bliss on the study of classification and the compilation of his own scheme with the very small number of libraries now using the scheme. It seems unlikely that many libraries will adopt it in the future, and yet so important is the study of classification made by Bliss that some account of his work on music must be given.

One of the most interesting features of BC is the lengthy discussion of the problems of classifying music. This can be found in the introduction to volume three, chapter five, section 3 and in the introductory material to class VV. Briefly, it may be said that Bliss is concerned with what the term 'music' means basically and to different people. He shows that music has many meanings such as 'sound', 'composition', 'rendition'. He is aware of the cross classification which is implicit in such concepts as 'singing a song' as opposed to 'the song that is sung'.

To turn to the schedules, MUSIC is in class V—AESTHETIC ARTS at VV. A synopsis can be found at the beginning of VV which gives a very clear picture of how the subject is organized.

As with LC and BCM, music scores and music literature are clearly separated:

vv—vw Music literature
vx Scores and Records

In a note under vx Bliss does suggest that the two can be combined at vv, but he obviously does not favour this. Records can go at vx5 and, if wished can be simplified in the same way as the scores. It is unlikely that any gramophone librarian would want to do this.

As in other parts of BC, alternative treatment is allowed in some divisions. For example, biography (vv9) may be arranged alphabetically by composer subdivided by a systematic schedule (no 7) provided at L9 BIOGRAPHY. This is not so detailed as the table for Wagner in LC but is more practical and can be applied easily to any composer. It might well be used for division of biographical material even if the BC scheme as a whole is not adopted. Alternatively biography can be arranged by country, subdivided alphabetically, or the arrangement can be chronological. In either case general systematic schedules for the *space* and *time* facets are provided.

The facets *techniques, elements* and *forms* all come together in a somewhat confused way under the general head :

VWD   Arts of composing and producing music

so that under

VWF   Composition (*technique*)

come such *elements* as

VWFB   Notation

VWFC   Staff

while under

VWI   Counterpoint (*element*)

come

VWIL   Fugue (*form*)

VWIP   Polyphonic music (to judge by definitions in dictionaries of music this is an imprecise term, but counterpoint is a subdivision of polyphony).

It must be apparent from the examples that the notation as in BCM and LC, is not expressive. The relationship of subjects as shown in these examples is based on the layout of the schedules.

Having dealt with the art of composition, Bliss next brings in STUDY and TEACHING, followed by PUBLICATION AND RECORDING OF MUSIC, then VOCAL AND INSTRUMENTAL MUSIC. His arrangement here is curious :

Under

VWU   Wind instruments

come VWUN   Percussion instruments

VWUU   Chamber music

VWUV   String quartets

The philosophical approach is seen in his arrangement of vocal music before instrumental music. He also makes provision for completely separate classes :

VWW   Religious music

VWY   Popular music

Is it possible to have religious instrumental music? No, as Bliss recognizes by not separating the music into religious and secular scores; but he does provide this place for literature discussing the subject. JAZZ comes under ORCHESTRAL MUSIC and not under POPULAR MUSIC.

The scores at VX are arranged :

36

VXH   Vocal scores
VXI   Duets
VXJ   Concert and chamber
VXK   Religious
VXL   Dramatic and operatic
VXM   Orchestral music
VXN   Chamber music
VXO—VXY   Individual instruments
Schedule 22 under PIANO can be used to subdivide any instrument:
VXP   Piano
VXPI   Piano sonatas (schedule 22)
VXT   Flute
Apply schedule 22:
VXTI   Flute sonata

This schedule provides a very simple way of dealing with composite subjects. Incidentally, the form CONCERTO will be found under both VXM and schedule 22. It is not indicated in the schedules, but presumably full scores are put under ORCHESTRA and arrangements for solo instrument and piano go under the instrument.

It would not be reasonable with this scheme, any more than with LC, to apply facet techniques to criticism of the arrangement of music literature, but once again a facet formula would be useful in using the scheme. However, commenting on the arrangement of scores, Dr Ranganathan's theories can be used, as Bliss has clearly applied these. The main tables are arranged by *instrument* and are subdivided by schedule 22 to give *form*. Thus in dealing with composite subjects the facet formula is clearly: instruments form.

The facet *size* is covered by VXN, although here instruments other than strings receive rather poor treatment.

This scheme reveals very careful thought behind its construction. Unfortunately the layout of the schedules gives evidence of haste. There is no symbol for guitar scores, for example, although provision is made for the instrument under the literature. It seems likely that this scheme, unlike that other excellent classification, the subject classification of James Duff Brown, will receive both regular and systematic revision. This is good, for it has much to commend it, and with revision its simple arrangement of scores would be most effective. Its notation, by using letters in preference to figures, can express composite subjects briefly.

DEWEY DECIMAL CLASSIFICATION SIXTEENTH EDITION

This is the most widely used scheme in the English-speaking world, and can be seen in use in most public libraries in Great Britain and America. Unfortunately, while it has much to commend it as a general scheme of classification, its treatment of music is such as to make some modification of the arrangement necessary in practice.

Its most obvious fault is the failure to separate literature and scores clearly. The most it does is to give a separate number for each within the same division:

787·1   Literature on the violin
787·15   Violin scores

Yet, curiously, bibliographies of books about music (classed with all other bibliographies at 016) are separated quite distinctly from bibliographies of scores at 781·97.

781   Theory and technique of music, reveals some rather unhappy arrangement. The definitions and scope notes given under specific class numbers in DC are often helpful. At least they make clear the intentions of the scheme. The difficulty comes sometimes in the conflict between what the librarian feels to be the organization of the subject in practice and its arrangement in the scheme:

781·2   Principles of music
781·22   Acoustics
              Including scales, intervals, tonalities, chords, pitch
781·4   Counterpoint
781·41   Melody
              Including twelve tone technique, quarter tones.

In this scheme the notation is expressive. It must be assumed therefore, that the compilers intend melody to be a subdivision of counterpoint, although it is not in practice so limited. Quarter tones would be better classed at acoustics, while twelve tone technique is surely a method of composition and should be under 781·61. It is also difficult to see why rhythm and metre are placed under composition, while harmony is accepted as a main division. The arrangement proceeds:

782   Dramatic music. (As literature and scores come together in DC librettos are arranged here with the scores. In other schemes they are separated.)

783   Sacred music. (Books about sacred instrumental music are classed here. The scores go with the instrument.)

784   Vocal music
785   Music for ensembles
786-9 Instrumental music.

One of the most curious features here is separation of the different forms of music for symphony orchestra:

785·1   Symphony orchestra and its music
    ·11   Symphonies
    ·12   Band and its music

·3   Small or light orchestra
         Including jazz
·5   Independent overtures for symphony orchestra
·6   Concertos
·7   Chamber music
·8   Suites for symphony orchestra.
A library would be quite justified in rearranging this section to bring all the music for symphony orchestra together.

Under 785·7 provision is made for the application of the *size* facet where instruments from different families are involved:
785·72   Duets
         Divide like 786-789 using the number for the instrument which appears first in a table of precedence on page 987 under 784-789.

Comprehensive works on musical instruments are placed at 781·91 and not at 786, which seems an unfortunate separation.

Under piano and organ, but not under other instruments, it is possible to express *form*. The method of dividing other instruments is set out under the violin (787·1). Where two or more instruments of the same kind are involved, entry is made under the instrument and not at 785·7:

Piano trio 785·7371 (Violin 787·1)

Trio for three clarinets 788·62543 (not 785·73862).

One disadvantage of this scheme as far as a separate music library is concerned is that it cannot be purchased, or used, separately. The arrangement seems more confused than in the other schemes examined. The facet order for scores is: instrument/size or form.

It does not seem to be possible to express both size and form, nor is it possible to express form for all instruments.

DEWEY DECIMAL CLASSIFICATION SEVENTEENTH EDITION

The sixteenth edition of DC was used as the main basis of this examination, for this is the edition most likely to be in use, but the seventeenth edition has been published recently and some comment is necessary on the changes which have been made.

Perhaps the most disappointing feature of the new edition is the lack of any fundamental change in the basic arrangement; literature and scores are still arranged together. On the other hand, several smaller features have been tidied up and others have been introduced. Some of the new elements show the influence of Dr Ranganathan's teaching. For example phase relationships can now be expressed at:

780·08   Relationship to literature and other arts

780·09   Relationships to subjects other than arts. 780·09 is completely new, while 780·08 formerly went with

780·07   Music and society, which is still retained in the new edition.

781·4   Counterpoint and

781·41   Melody, have been reversed to give the better chain

781·4   Melody and counterpoint

781·41   Counterpoint.

Bibliographies of the literature (016·78 or 780·16) and of the scores (781·97) are still separated, although there has been a reshuffle at 781·97, the advantage of which is not immediately apparent.

The printing and publishing of music (781·98) has now been moved to 655 under the general subject of printing. In a general library this is reasonable but a special music library will probably want to retain 781·98.

785   (Instrumental ensembles and their music) has been rearranged so that books about the ensembles are separated within 785 from the music :

785·0661   Full symphony orchestra

785·11   Symphonies for orchestra

Under the general class 785, various special subdivisions are listed; these can be applied to the different forms of music for ensembles. For example, a book on the symphony orchestra will be placed at 785·0661, an analysis of the symphony at 785·11015 (015 =analytical guides from the special subdivisions), and scores of the symphonies at 785·115. This means that, while books on the orchestra are separated from the scores, books on the symphony itself are not. This seems rather confusing and could be avoided by a complete separation of music and literature as in other schemes.

788·7   (Double reed instruments in the sixteenth edition) has been designated ' Oboe and English horn ', but the coverage remains the same. This is indicative of the form of many of the changes in class 780 which are sometimes more apparent than real.

It is almost a pity that this scheme is used by so many music libraries. This is not to deny its usefulness or its historical importance; when it was first published it was revolutionary in its conception, but like other revolutions it has become outmoded by the passage of time and events. While recognizing this, many librarians are understandably reluctant to change.

THE MCCOLVIN SCHEME

The task of reclassifying a library is a large one, but if librarians feel unable to undertake this work for the whole library they may find it possible at least for the music class, for which Lionel McColvin devised a special scheme using the decimal notation. This was originally printed in his book *Music libraries* published in 1937 (Grafton) and reprinted in the new edition revised by Jack Dove in 1965 (Deutsch). It is this scheme which influenced the formation of BCM and is in use at the Central Music Library in London. It is a very simple scheme and has much to commend it to the librarian who is dissatisfied with DC but not prepared to use BCM.

Music is classed at 780-782, while the literature occupies the rest of the division (*ie* 783-789). Vocal music comes first at 780 and is subdivided into secular and sacred. Secular songs are arranged according to the number of voices.

780·3   Songs by individual composers, A-Z
780·41 Duets—mixed voices—by composer, A-Z
780·42 Duets—female voices—by composer, A-Z
etc
780·44 Trios, quartets etc also subdivided by type of voice and then by composer, A-Z

Sacred music is arranged by form.

Instrumental music (solo and duet) is arranged in the order: wind, string (*ie* plucked), bowed, keyboard. Music for piano and another instrument goes under the other instrument, but music for two instruments, neither of which is the piano, is placed under the one with the higher average compass or the less common where they have comparable compass. This is a curious method. Surely it is easier to have an automatic rule such as placing under the one listed first in the schedules. Solos and duets are followed by chamber music and orchestral music. Miniature scores are arranged separately at 782·99 with no indication of the sub-arrangement in the outline schedules, although in volume two of *Music libraries* they are arranged alphabetically by composers. (Incidentally the running title 'music scores' in volume two of this work which continues to 789·98 must be a misprint and should be ignored.)

Opera appears at 780·7 quite conveniently separated from other secular vocal music to place it near instrumental music with which it is closely associated. If this was the reason for this arrangement, it is difficult to understand why the order of sacred and secular under vocal music was not reversed, to give the order:

780   Sacred music
780·5   Solo vocal music
780·7   Opera
781   Instrumental music

Arrangements are always classified under the instrument for which the piece is arranged, with no attempt to specify the original instrument. Nor is any attempt made to specify form under individual instruments. It is claimed by Jack Dove (page 48 of new edition) that it is nearly impossible to separate forms, but this is not really so in the case of clearly defined forms where the composer has deliberately written in a form such as sonata. To separate here would appear to be useful, especially where the material available is as numerous as is the music for piano.

With the addition of places for the foci in such facets as *elements, forms, space* and *time* the literature section follows the same order as that for the music. It is a simpler and much better arranged classification for the literature than that provided in DC. It is unfortunate that the new editions of both schemes still fail to make any adequate provision for the literature of jazz. McColvin has dance band, dance music, jazz, swing and pops all at 786·9 with no attempt at subdivision. The inclusion of these very different forms under the one head is an indication of lack of understanding of this important division of music, in which research is as detailed and as busy as elsewhere. To the specialist it is as foolish to class jazz and pops together as it is to place opera and the mass in the same division.

However this is a practical scheme designed to offer a substitute for the confusion which abounds in class 780 of DC, and in this it succeeds admirably. In the section on DC not too much emphasis has been placed on the failings of the American scheme as these are self evident on the shelves of most of the public libraries in this country. It is perhaps sufficient criticism that Lionel McColvin found it necessary to devise his own scheme and that the resulting improvement in the arrangement is immediately evident, whatever minor criticisms there may be of the McColvin scheme. It would be interesting to know why the DC editorial board has not adopted this or some similar scheme in place of the existing DC class. Such a radical improvement would add real value to a new edition.

ALTERNATIVE METHODS OF ARRANGEMENT

It is the practice of some libraries, particularly on the continent, to arrange their collections according to the systematic arrangement used in some of the standard bibliographies of music. It is not proposed to deal at any length with these schemes, as this method is unlikely to be used in this country where the majority of librarians seem to prefer a scheme devised by a classificationist rather than one developed by a musicologist. As the latters' schemes seem to differ from each other as frequently as do the formers', the librarian is as likely to find difficulty with one of these schemes as he is with one of the traditionally acceptable classifications.

However, the BBC has recently begun publication of the catalogues of its music library; and, as it has used, for the classified index to its *Chamber music catalogue,* a modified form of the classification devised by Wilhelm Altmann for his *Kammermusik-Katalog,* it may be convenient to examine this arrangement as typical of those offered by the bibliographies of music, further details of which are provided in the bibliography on page 77. There is no notation, but one could easily be provided if required.

Group I is CHAMBER MUSIC WITHOUT KEYBOARD. This is arranged by size of ensemble from septets, octets etc, to duos. Each size is subdivided into strings, strings and wind, wind. From quintets downwards the division is more precise, allowing under quintets, for example, for:

2 violins, 2 violas, cello *or*
2 violins, viola, 2 cellos.

and under quartets for 4 violins, 4 violas or 4 cellos as well as the more usual combinations.

Group II is CHAMBER MUSIC WITH KEYBOARD, which employs very nearly the same principles of division allowing for the different kinds of ensemble met in this group. Thus under trios:

keyboard, violin, viola
keyboard, violin, cello
keyboard, 2 violins
keyboard, 2 cellos
keyboard, string, wind
keyboard, wind
keyboard, miscellaneous.

Under duos comes the very large number of sonatas for keyboard and other instruments, although sonata is not specified in the classification.

Group III is VOICES WITHOUT KEYBOARD. Once again basic division is by size:

two or more voices with various accompaniment
voice with string quartet
voice with three strings or wind
voice with two strings or wind
voice with single string or wind

Group IV is VOICE WITH KEYBOARD, very similarly arranged. Group V, SELECTED INSTRUMENTS WITH ACCOMPANIMENT, is rather curiously named as it includes guitar and harp solos as well as such divisions as harp and clarinet, percussion with instruments and baryton trios (*viz* those by Haydn). The principle of selection is not explained, but this group seems to include those instruments not normally found in a symphony orchestra as frequently as those not selected. Although this principle seems false when Group VI,

SELECTED SOLO INSTRUMENTS, while including the normal instruments of a symphony orchestra, includes bagpipe, coach-horn and regal.

The BBC Music Library is one of the finest collections of music in the world and has probably been used by most of the world's greatest musicians. Its choice of a classification must therefore be founded on considerable practical experience. This scheme based on Altmann does seem good in its broad outline and in its use of the *size* facet as a primary means of division, but it becomes very muddled in its last two groups, as has been shown. In fact it would surely be simpler to have one group only for solo instrument and to place such items as Haydn's baryton trios under trios, which is where they logically belong in a scheme arranged by size.

In a paper read at the IAML conference at Cambridge in 1959 Dr Alfons Ott suggested a very simple classification for scores which small libraries might find useful (see *Music, libraries and instruments* page 77). In this, instrumental music is divided to provide places for scores according to the quantity a small library is likely to have. Thus, piano music is divided into solo, duet and two pianos, while wind music is divided only into woodwind, brass, recorder and chamber music in which wind features. Orchestral music is divided simply into full and miniature scores. This scheme is commended for its simplicity to librarians who have only a small collection.

It must be apparent that all the schemes, whatever their origin, use as arranging devices one or more of the facets isolated in chapter one. It cannot be emphasized too strongly that the choice of a scheme must depend on the approach that the majority of readers will make. Only when this is known can the scheme be selected. It is important to remember that a scheme such as BCM combines the experience of music librarians with the scientific approach of the classificationist.

CHAPTER FOUR

Cataloguing: author and description

IT IS NOT THE INTENTION to discuss here all problems met in dealing with a collection of music, but only those which are peculiar to the form, or are especially difficult when encountered in music. It is obvious, for example, that the basic problems of authors' names will be the same for music as for any other subject, with the addition that, because music is not dependent on language for its understanding, foreign names occur more frequently than they do in other subjects. Furthermore, the whole problem of the author catalogue in music has been so fully discussed by Franz Grasberger in volume one of the *Code international de catalogage de la musique* that the reader cannot do better than refer to his study, which has been adequately translated by Virginia Cunningham in parallel columns to the original German text. Extensive references are given to enable the enthusiast to pursue the subject along his own independent lines of enquiry.

There have been many attempts to provide libraries with a cataloguing code for music, of which two have been selected for treatment here because they are easily accessible at present and both in print. One is the *Code for cataloging music and phonorecords,* which was prepared by a joint committee of the American Music Library Association and the American Library Association. The second is the one mentioned above, of which Franz Grasberger's work forms the first volume and which is being produced by the International Association of Music Libraries. Unfortunately the latter is still in progress and so far only the first two volumes have been published. The second volume is a limited *Code,* which will be found very useful by librarians without a knowledge of music who are faced with the problem of cataloguing music scores. It is difficult to find information about the contents of the complete *Code* but it would seem that it is intended to cover full cataloguing, cataloguing of manuscripts and of gramophone records.

The American *Code* was published in 1958, but is really dated 1949 for the most part, since chapter one 'Entry' was published as rule number 12 of the American Library Association's *Cataloging rules for author and title entries* (second edition 1949), while chapter two, 'Description' is the same as chapter nine of the *Rules for descriptive cataloging* issued by the Library of Congress in 1949. Chapter three, 'Phonorecords' is the same as chapter nine (a) of the Congress *Rules*. There has been some alteration in style in the later publication, while there are additional chapters giving simplified rules and filing rules for conventional titles. The volume is completed by a glossary.

The problems of cataloguing music literature are the same as those to be solved in dealing with the subject literature in any other discipline. It is music scores which present difficulties. Unfortunately some librarians without knowledge of the subject assume that music librarians are creating problems unnecessarily, and proceed to catalogue the scores in their libraries without reference to the solutions suggested by subject specialists, and apparently without considering the needs of their readers. It is hoped that the following survey of some of the difficulties likely to be encountered will at least make librarians aware of the need for specific attention to cataloguing in this field.

THE TITLE PAGE
A fundamental rule in all author cataloguing has in the past been to use the title page as the primary source of information about any particular book. It is doubtful now whether there is much validity in maintaining this rule for books, for publishers tend to give important information elsewhere in the volume; there is even less point to its use in cataloguing scores, where the title page is quite often irrelevant. Some typical situations are:

1 *Title page missing*: A very common practice with music publishers is to supply a work with a paper cover and without a title page. The information normally supplied on the title page is given either on the cover or on the first page of the score. This practice is followed by all types of firms. For example, in 1937 OUP published a piano arrangement of Walton's *Crown imperial,* for which there is no title page. Copyright details are given on the first page of the score, but there is no indication that it is a piano arrangement, except on the cover. In neither place is there information about the arranger.

46

There does not seem much point in using addition [ ] and omission . . . signs in general cataloguing, when describing modern printed books. There is even less point when the item, as in the case of a score, has no recognized title page. The simple solution would be to decide on an order in which the different parts of the catalogue entry are to be arranged, and to find the necessary information for each part wherever possible. The reader will surely trust the librarian to do his work honestly and will not be concerned with the source of the information provided.

Scores quite often receive rough physical treatment. This can mean that second-hand music which a library acquires may have lost its cover. Here again the same method can be employed, with possibly a note to indicate the source of any information supplied from bibliographies, although it is doubtful again whether the average reader is anxious to know the origin of any details. In handling a score, such as the example quoted above, when it has lost its cover, the non-musician cataloguer would be in some extra difficulty, for he has no indication of the true nature of the work *ie* that it is an arrangement. The only advice that can be given is to be suspicious of all scores, and to have adequate bibliographical resources available for checking.

2 *Title page in a foreign language*: The musician will usually possess many scores of his own besides those he borrows from a library. Among them will be some with title pages in foreign languages, but the music will be the same, with the directions probably in Italian. This situation arises from the international nature of music publishing, in which a publisher may issue the same score in several countries at the same time, the only variation being that the title page will be printed in the language appropriate to each country. Many publishers do not even bother to do this, but sell the same edition with the same title page wherever it is required. Even where they have used different title pages publishers quite frequently sell copies with different title pages in any one country, especially when an issue in one language has sold out.

Therefore, the librarian who orders a particular title may find he has the correct copy, but with the title page in a foreign language. For example, this work was found recently on the shelves of a small public library:—

Collection Litoff / Sonates / pour / piano et violon / DE /

W A Mozart / Nouvelle Edition / soigneusement revue par /

J N Rauch / Braunschweig / Henry Litoff's Verlag /.

The work is that of a German editor and publisher with a French title page in an English library! The mistake here would surely be to follow the title page. This would only result in the work being filed in the wrong place as far as users of the catalogue are concerned. Once again, the simplest solution would be to arrange the descriptive part of the entry in an agreed order, translating any foreign information into the home language of the library.

A minor problem with title pages in foreign languages is transliteration. Because of the frequency of works published abroad, the music librarian has to contend not only with transliteration into his own language, a problem which is, however, easily solved with the general aids such as the British Standard on transliteration, or more sensibly by following the forms used in *Grove* which every musician consults. He must also deal with the (to him) somewhat strange forms which transliterated names take in other foreign languages. Chatschaturjan may not be immediately recognisable as Khachaturian, nor Vorisek as Worzischek.

Another minor matter is the variation in the symbols or names used for the different keys in the major European languages. The English ' E flat major ' is represented in German by ' Es-dur ', and in France and Italy by ' mi bémol majeur '. The musician does not generally need to remember these differences, as he relies on the key signature to tell him the key of a piece. Therefore, if the cataloguer copies the title page it is not much help to the musician. The foreign terms must be translated into English if the catalogue is to inform the reader.

Sometimes a title page may have the title in more than one language. The international *Code* requires the title to be transcribed in all the languages and the rest in the original language. English libraries will probably prefer to use English in all cases.

3 *Title page listing several works*: Music publishers frequently issue scores with title pages listing several works, the title relevant to the particular score sometimes being underlined. For example there is an Augener edition of Schumann's *Etudes symphoniques,* opus 13 which lists, on what is supposedly the title page, all the piano works by that composer without any indication of the actual work contained therein. Presumably this is done so that the page can be easily used as an advertisement in other publications. Once again there is no point in following the title page.

4 *Title page order varies*: There is no agreed way of referring to music. This means that some title pages for a given work will have the form ' concerto for violin ', others ' violin concerto '. Which of the two a library selects must depend on the approach its readers generally make, but it would be unhelpful always to follow the title page.

5 *Arrangements*: A situation in which the title page is often irrelevant is the very common case where an arrangement of the

original piece has been made, either by simplifying it or by editing it for another instrument. The following is a particularly interesting example, where the title page reads:

To Sidney and Frances Colvin / Concerto / for / violoncello and orchestra / composed by / Edward Elgar / op 85 / Arrangement for violoncello and piano / by the composer /

This provides unusually complete information, or so it seems until the contents of the work are examined, to reveal that it is a second arrangement of this work for viola and piano by Lionel Tertis. It is only the viola part which supplies this information, for the piano part is scored for piano with the cello line shown.

6 *Title page omits essential information*: Some of the earlier examples serve to underline the lack of essential information on music title pages, but there are many situations where the items omitted are so important that it is difficult to understand why they are not included. This is particularly true where a transposing instrument such as the clarinet is involved. For example the A clarinet is scored for C major when the composer wishes it to sound in A major, while its close relative the B flat clarinet is scored for C major when the piece is in B flat major. The reasons for this are historical and complicated, but many players only possess a B flat instrument. It is vital therefore for the player to know for which instrument the music is arranged. A professional standard clarinettist can transpose as he plays, but not all players are that good and in any case this is really fundamental information about the score. Thus the following title page is incomplete:

Schumann / Fantasiestücke / für Klavier und Klarinette / oder violine / opus 73.

It does not say whether this is the arrangement for violin or clarinet, nor in the latter case does it say which instrument is required. In fact the piece was originally written for the A clarinet, but this particular score is for the B flat instrument. This can be confusing and does require care in cataloguing, if reliance on the title page can result in incomplete information.

7 *Title page without useful identifying elements*: In identifying a piece of music, three items are of great importance: opus number, number within a series, and thematic catalogue number. An imaginative title is also very useful with certain categories of composition such as opera, although the titles given to instrumental works by people other than the composer can often be confusing. Thus Berlioz's *Symphonie fantastique* can be quite safely identified by this title, but Haydn's *Mass* no 9 in D minor is most clearly identified by this title rather than the more popular 'Nelson', 'Imperial' or 'Coronation' by which it is generally known. Curiously here,

the composer in his own catalogue did use a title—*Missa in Angustiis*. The clearest identification is not always given, for sometimes (as in the case of the Haydn mass) the popular titles vary from country to country.

One of the safest methods of checking for details about a particular work is to use the thematic catalogue of the composer's works if one has been issued. Once the work has been identified the thematic catalogue number can be used in the catalogue entry even if the publisher has not supplied it. Failing a thematic catalogue, a collected edition of the composer's works is often useful, as also is the latest edition of *Grove* (1954, with supplementary volume 1961). Many of the composer articles in this admirable dictionary contain tabulated lists of the composer's works which can help in identification.

Opus numbers are very useful, but composers do not use them consistently. Bartok reached opus 20 and then appears to have tired of this system. Even then, according to the chronological list in the work on the composer by Halsey Stevens, this should have been numbered opus 57. Bartok was a very systematic composer, so it is no matter for surprise that other composers' opus numbers are even more confused and that they are used inconsistently by publishers. Nevertheless, if they exist, but are not given on the title page, they should be supplied in the catalogue entry.

Numbers of works in series (*eg* symphonies, quartets) are extremely useful, but are sometimes not supplied by publishers, or else are incorrectly given. Perhaps the best known example of the confusion which can occur here is in the symphonies of Dvořak, totalling nine, but until recently in this country thought to be only five. The discovery that there were four earlier symphonies has meant renumbering the later five. Consequently many libraries must have scores or recordings of two number fives. Publishers and record companies still sometimes ignore these developments, so that care is needed to ensure correct numbering.

Another common trap is Schubert's symphony no 9, quite frequently identified as no 7. Many references to the earliest quartet by Haydn refer to it as 'no o' as it did not appear in the original list, Haydn himself having classified it as a divertimento. Anthony van Hoboken in his thematic catalogue of Haydn's works has kept it as a divertimento. The Hoboken thematic catalogue number is now the safest identification even if the designation 'string quartet' is used: string quartet, HV II 6. The designation 'Op 1, no o' can be inserted as a further means of identification. Sometimes publishers refer to this work as 'Op 1, no 1' but this should be used for another earlier work in B flat. The American *Code* suggests giving both opus numbers in cases of conflict, showing the name of the publisher first using each number.

This matter has been discussed at some length because some cataloguers assume too readily that it is easy to identify music by means of opus and series numbers.

8 *Imaginative titles*: The cataloguer of literature faces the problem of the variety of translated titles for the same literary work. Music offers peculiar difficulties in that quite often a work will be known equally well by its original and its translated title. Some works are known by the original titles, others by a generally accepted translation. Compare *The magic flute, La clemenza di Tito, The merry wives of Windsor, Così fan tutte* and *The nutcracker* or *Casse-noisette*. No one has been able to find a common pattern to these, which might offer the basis for a common solution.

The American *Code* requires the use of the foreign title if the original language is one of the languages most commonly read in America. These are English, French, German, Italian, Spanish, Portuguese and Latin. If the title is in a language other than one of these, the title in most common use in the United States is to be used. Other factors being equal, the English title is to be preferred. This would seem to work as a rule, but it is immediately possible to think of titles such as *Le nozze di Figaro* for which it seems less than good. It would probably be better to leave the whole thing to the discretion of the cataloguer, who could base his decision on the general practice in encyclopedias, monographs, periodicals etc. The American *Code* suggests this for discovering the title in most common use in the United States, when the original is in one of the less common foreign languages. In its ' Simplified rules ' this *Code* recommends using the English title.

A somewhat similar situation arises in the cases of songs such as *Lieder* and folk songs. With the former there is generally a variety of translated titles, and it is much better here to group them under the title in the original language when that is French, German, Italian, Spanish or Latin; songs in other languages would be grouped under the most generally accepted English title. Folk songs are not collected by all libraries, but where they are and the different titles represent the same work, it is probably best to group them under the title in most general use. Where the songs are distinct variants of each other, each title should be used with linking references.

All the above problems are met in dealing with the title pages of music scores. Against some, the solution suggested by the two major *Codes* has been reported. Both offer general solutions which attempt to dispose of problems effectively.

The international *Code* mentions (page 20) the three titles between which there is a choice, *viz* cover title, main title and caption title (found on the first page of the music). Preference is given to the main title; if there is none, the most complete of the others should be used. It does not permit any inversion of the elements of the title, although it does allow omissions with the appropriate sign. Additions must be made using the conventional sign and are recommended for the type, key, medium, physical format, opus and thematic catalogue numbers.

In a later section (page 39) it goes on to discuss the problem raised as point four above (see page 48). In order not to have the same work scattered throughout one composer's sequence under such forms as 'concerto for violin', 'Konzert für Violine' and 'violin concerto', it suggests a classified arrangement under composers with a large output: complete works; theatrical works; vocal works; instrumental works; pedagogical works; cross references.

Within each of these it will be necessary to provide a sub-arrangement such as instrument or form under instrumental works.

The international *Code* mentions (page 39) the solution, adopted by the American *Code* for all the title problems met in cataloguing music, namely the use of a conventional title. This is simply a filing title which is used in order to identify a work and to bring together different editions of that work. It is obviously necessary to be very systematic in the forming of a conventional title, and an important part of the American *Code* (pages 14-30) consists of rules for this (also to be found in *Rules for descriptive cataloging,* pages 75-88). Some idea of the form a conventional title takes can be gained from these typical entries:

Beethoven, Ludwig van.
　　[Concerto, piano, no 1, op 15, c major]
　　Piano concerto no 1.
Verdi, Giuseppe.
　　[Aida. Celeste Aida]
　　Celeste Aida
Bach, Johann Sebastian.
　　[Concerto, harpsichord & string orchestra, S.
　　1056, f minor; arr.]
　　Violin concerto, in g minor.

As can be seen, the titles found on the title pages are given after the conventional titles. This is certainly an effective compromise between the views of those requiring a standardized entry and those preferring to follow traditional cataloguing methods in giving the title exactly as it appears on the title page. There is no reason why a cataloguer should not take this a stage further and use only the conventional title; the title page title can be added when required for essential information, but, in public libraries particularly, all the musician requires is the identification of the work and not an accurate description of the title page. Where it is desired to express the edition, the editor's name or any other suitable element can be added to the conventional title; which in this practice need not appear in square brackets:

Haydn, Franz Josef.
    Sonatas, piano, edited by Christa Landon.

Imprint details and series note will also help in identification.

This last method is not recommended, of course, for scores printed or in manuscript before 1800, nor is it recommended for scholarly libraries. It is suitable for the library where most readers want something to play and their main interest is either composer, form or instrument. If it is necessary to catalogue scores quickly, while still giving some attention to traditional methods, the simplified rules in the American *Code* are worth considering.

THE HEADING IN A COMPOSER CATALOGUE

All the problems discussed so far in this chapter have been concerned with the title page. Other parts of the entry do present some difficulties, and in solving the two basic questions in deciding the heading to be adopted, 'Under whom as author?' and 'Under what form of name?', the general cataloguing code in use in the general departments of a multi-subject library can be used whenever suitable. However, there are situations in music which it may not meet; in such a case, and certainly in a specialist music library, the two music codes will be found useful.

1 *Form of composer's name*: As far as the form of name is concerned, one very simple solution is to follow *Grove*. The BBC has done this in its music library catalogues. This practice has much to commend it, particularly as most musicians are familiar with *Grove*.

It is American cataloguing practice to give the full name, together with dates of birth and death. This is not really essential, except where it is necessary to distinguish between two composers with the same name. Most composers are referred to quite simply by their surnames: Beethoven, Bach, Monteverdi, Schoenberg, Britten. There does not seem to be anything against using this simple identifying element as a heading in a composer catalogue. There is really no need in a catalogue to head every Mozart entry with: Mozart, Johann Chrysostom Wolfgang Amadeus, 1756-1791. This does not really identify him more clearly than: Mozart.

In the case of the Bach family it would have the advantage of bringing the most important member of the family to the front of the Bach sequence—the one universally identified by the name Bach:

Bach

Bach, Carl Philipp Emanuel

Bach, Johann Christian, etc.

2 *Arrangements*: This general term is to cover the many ways in which one composer has worked on the music of another, covering such phrases as 'adaptations', 'reduction', 'fantasy on', 'variations on' etc. The international *Code* offers two solutions to the problem raised here, as to which composer's name should be used for the heading. One is a scientific distinction which will be found in volume one (pages 36-38), while the other is a completely mechanical rule given in the second volume (pages 18-19), which non-musician cataloguers will find quite adequate for most situations. The American *Code* (rules IA11 and IA12) does require a knowledge of music for satisfactory use, as the cataloguer is instructed to examine such items as the harmony and the thematic material. F Grasberger in the first volume of the international *Code* also requires a musical examination of the text. There is a careful analysis of the different types of arrangement and some useful examples. The use of the three rules does not always result in the same solution. For example, in dealing with *pot-pourri,* Grasberger suggests the solution will depend on the kind of combinations, and his examples suggest that, where there is no change in the basic instrumentation, entry will be under the original composer. The international *Limited code* has the mechanical rule requiring entry under the arranger, while the American *Code* places *pot-pourris* from one composer under the original composer.

CADENZAS

It is curious once again to find disagreement between the first two volumes of the international *Code*. The *Limited code* requires entry under the composer of the cadenza when it has been published separately. Grasberger gives no examples, but states quite emphatically that entry must be made under the composer of the concerto. The American *Code* agrees with Grasberger. Entry under the original composer does seem the more logical, even in the extreme case of equal fame such as a Beethoven cadenza to a Mozart concerto.

LIBRETTOS

This type of text, where the words are separated from the music with which they are normally associated, needs to be carefully distinguished from a vocal score which contains both music and words. In the latter case there is really no problem, as entry can be quite simply made under the composer. But in entering librettos, cataloguers are faced with the problem that the writer of the words is quite clearly responsible for the literary content of the text, but the work will probably be known and sought by the name of the composer.

Comment has already been made on some of the classification schemes' treatment of librettos, but a comparative list is provided here since it does have some bearing:

BCM: Class B under composer with literature on the composer.
LC: Class ML48—ML54 under composer, except those published before 1800 which are arranged by title.
BC: VWSP with books on opera *or* VXL5 with the scores, then apparently to be arranged by nationality of the composer.
DC: 782·12 with books and scores. No indication on sub-arrangement.

Both the special schemes arrange under composer. Particularly interesting is the special arrangement in LC for operas before 1800. Grasberger (page 16) draws attention to the wide variation in cataloguing practice, some codes suggesting composer and others author, and recommends entry under title for librettos of all periods. It is doubtful whether this solution would be acceptable to the majority of British and American librarians, as it contradicts the fundamental rule of cataloguing, that a work is entered under the name of the person responsible for the intellectual content. However, it has much to commend it, particularly in the context of Grasberger's further suggestion that a separate catalogue of librettos should be maintained arranged in title order.

THEMATIC CATALOGUES

There is really no problem here in the material itself, but a difficulty has been created by the curious instruction in the 1908 Anglo-American *Code* that thematic catalogues of a composer's works are to be entered under the composer. This has been quite correctly reversed in the ALA *Code* and the American *Music code*. Entry under the composer is a subject entry, and, while it is probably true that most searches for such items will begin under the composer's name, to prescribe entry under subject in an author catalogue contradicts the fundamental rule mentioned above. The variation from a basic principle is more drastic and less wise in this situation than the decision to enter librettos under the title, as compilers of thematic catalogues do tend to be better known for their work than are librettists.

The problem of both thematic catalogues and librettists does raise the question of the validity of the main entry in cataloguing. There are many situations where it is just not possible to decide who is principally responsible for the content of a work; in such situations it would seem better to follow the practice of double entry under both names. For thematic catalogues one entry is, as has been stated, a subject entry, but the principle of double entry could be used for such items in an author catalogue and generally for arrangements of all kinds, cadenzas and librettos. Libraries using the unit card method could use the descriptive part of the entry as the basic unit without deciding on a main heading. When the material is arranged on the shelves by a classification scheme it seems an unnecessary refinement to have a main entry with unit cards in use. This is a small point perhaps, but a lot of time is spent cumulatively, even in just typing main entry headings, apart from time spent on choice where it is allowed for a main entry.

DESCRIPTION OF SCORES

1 *Transcript of title page*: The transcription of the title page has been dealt with in discussing the whole problem of the title pages of music scores. Some librarians feel very strongly that the catalogue entry must reproduce the title page accurately and there are occasions, especially in describing early music, when this is essential. But there is no agreement among publishers on the way this page should be organized, and some information which used to be given on the title page is now given on the back, while some titles are spread across two pages. In these circumstances the slavish reproduction of the title page in a catalogue entry can only make use of the catalogue more difficult. The real solution lies with the publishers, who could surely agree on the information essential to their title pages and the order in which it is to be given. Even within such rules there would still be room for the variations needed to create a house style.

2 *Imprint*: The information given in the imprint for music scores is basically the same as that for books, with the addition of the plate number. This very useful serial number can be used as a means of identifying the edition, if nothing else serves. Most libraries seem to agree that this item belongs to the imprint, as do both the American *Code* and Grasberger. The international *Limited Code,* on the other hand, recommends placing it in the collation. There are reasons for both rulings. It is a reference number for publisher and printer, thereby linking it with the physical make up of the book and the collation. It can equally well be claimed as an

extension of the publisher's name, since this or his initials are usually included within the symbol.

While cataloguing codes require the imprint to include place of publication, publisher and date, there is a very great variation in practice from one library to another. The international nature of music does make the place of publication seem unimportant, but the name of the publisher quite often indicates the style of printing etc, and could therefore be counted a useful item. The date, when it is easily found, is certainly valuable if comparison between copies of the same work is needed. The international *Code* gives the most useful rule for this section of the imprint, although the Bibliothèque Nationale has the best approach: ' If an imprint must be given, give it in French and justify it in a note '.

3 *Collation*: Unfortunately, the French do not have such a useful rule for this part of the description. The essential information is not how many pages and what type of illustrations, but what type of score it is and the size, if it is unusual, for the particular kind of music, causing it to be shelved apart from the rest of its kind.

Thus some typical collations might be: full score; score and parts; vocal score; piano score; miniature score.

The various kinds of score are defined in the glossary under ' score '. If it is desired to transcribe the title page exactly and this information is given in that part of the description, there is no point in repeating it here. If a systematic order is followed, this is the most useful place for such information. The two main codes follow the traditional approach in this section, but the international *Code* does allow the use of such symbols as 8° and 4° to indicate the size, while the American *Code* agrees with general Anglo-American practice in expressing it in centimetres, which does not convey very much to most readers. At least the conventional symbols can be defined in a guide to the use of the catalogue.

4 *Notes*: The American *Code* provides some useful guidance on the kind of notes which should be given, while the international *Code* has very little to say. Probably the best rule is to leave the whole matter to the cataloguer, to give in the form of notes any additional information which he feels will be useful.

CHAPTER FIVE

Subject cataloguing

THE MAIN PROBLEM REMAINING to be discussed is the method of satisfying the enquiry by subject or form. There has been and is endless discussion about the relative merits of the classified and dictionary catalogues, and therefore the only consideration here will be to see what each can provide by way of solution to the kind of subject or form enquiries which a music librarian receives.

It is probably true to say that each kind of catalogue will have advantages for certain types of music library. Some will decide, for example, that by far the greater number of their enquiries are made by using the name of the composer as the basic item of information, and therefore there is very little point in providing anything else beyond a composer catalogue. The only point where the problem of arrangement will arise is under voluminous composers, where some division of their work becomes necessary. For this the arrangement suggested by the international *Code* seems entirely suitable. This was discussed in the previous chapter (see page 52).

The classified or dictionary catalogues have their uses immediately it is obvious that readers are going to make more than one kind of approach to the material on the shelves. Music departments of larger libraries may well have their decisions dictated by the kind of catalogue in use throughout that library, but where freedom of choice is possible the following may serve as some guide.

CLASSIFIED CATALOGUE
The advantage of the classified catalogue lies mainly in the systematic way in which the catalogue can be organized, especially when some technique such as chain indexing is used. Alphabetical order

is not as simple as ABC, as the existence of complicated filing rules proves. The use of symbols, provided by a classification scheme, to arrange entries in a catalogue does simplify the whole filing procedure. Alphabetical order does become necessary, however, within each class number and in arranging the composer/author/title and subject indexes, but in all the latter, if they are arranged separately, the problem of alphabetization is less acute.

The merit of the classified catalogue does depend to some extent on the classification scheme on which it is based, but presumably the latter will have been chosen for the order it produces on the shelves and, if that is desirable in arranging the material, it will be equally useful in the catalogue. The classified catalogue, when used with the chain indexing technique, does reveal a variety of supplementary orders in the alphabetical subject index. This is achieved with all classification schemes, but it is shown to the best advantage with a faceted scheme such as BCM, where a sample taken at random reveals the following:

Classified file:

QPE	Piano sonatas
RE	Organ sonatas
SPE	Violin & piano sonatas
WTE	Horn sonatas

Subject index:

Sonatas	:	Horn	WTE
Sonatas	:	Organ	RE
Sonatas	:	Piano	QPE
Sonatas	:	Violin & piano	SPE

In this example, the classification scheme has separated the form sonatas because the primary facet in this scheme is *executant,* which is subdivided by the *form* facet. By using the chain indexing technique, each focus in the subordinate facets can be brought together in the alphabetical arrangement to reveal other orders and thereby meet other lines of enquiry. The other elements are revealed very simply by the chain from the main class to the specific number for a particular subject:

BBC	Bach
AR	Organ
A/Y	Fugue
A/RM	Counterpoint
BBCAR/Y/RM	Bach's counterpoint in his organ fugues.

From that chain it is possible to make the following index entries simply by indexing each essential step in turn:

59

Counterpoint : Fugues : Organ : Bach	BBCAR/Y/RM
Fugues : Organ : Bach	BBCAR/Y
Organ : Bach	BBCAR
Bach	BBC

In indexing it is simplest to proceed from the most specific point in the chain to the broadest. At each link in the chain the element in the symbol representing the previous lower link is removed. Thus at

Fugues : Organ : Bach   BBCAR/Y

the /RM for counterpoint is removed. Each of these index entries will, of course, be arranged in alphabetical order in the subject index.

By making these index entries, various other approaches to the material have been met, different from the basic one selected by the classification scheme. Thus in the BCM the material is arranged by composer, but the index supplies arrangements by instrument, form and element. Presumably the majority of readers will be satisfied by the composer order on the shelves, if the classification scheme has been carefully selected with the needs of most readers in mind, but the person interested in counterpoint will be guided to this book by the index, even though it is not arranged with other books on the subject at A/RM.

This method of compiling a catalogue does have advantages with music, as the subject can be broken up fairly neatly into its component facets, even when the subjects the books deal with are fairly complex. To use the catalogue the reader does not need any knowledge of chain indexing technique. It does not reveal to him immediately the presence of a book on

Bach : Organ : Fugues : Counterpoint

but if he does search in this way, as he might, then the entry under Bach will take him to an appropriate starting point in the classified sequence. If this sequence is adequately guided, as indeed it must be as a part of this method, then he will have no difficulty in finding the particular aspect of Bach's work he wishes to study. The simplicity of this drill can be tested quite easily by using one of the annual volumes of the *British catalogue of music*. It will be noted that this bibliography arranges the alphabetical section of the catalogue in one sequence of authors, composers, titles and subjects, but there is nothing to prevent a librarian from having separate sequences for these if he so desires.

The chain indexing technique can be used nearly as effectively with the enumerative schemes, as this example from LC will show :

M5 —M1459	Instrumental music	
M6 —M176	Solo	
M6 —M39		Keyboard

M20—M39   Piano
M23   Sonatas

Index:
Sonatas : Piano	M23
Piano solos	M20—M39
Keyboard instruments	M6 —M39
Solos : Instrumental music	M6 —M176
Instrumental music	M

As can be seen, the method has to be adapted slightly and care must be taken to see that each step in the chain is enumerated. In indexing, natural phrases should be used wherever appropriate :

Piano solos

rather than

Piano : Solos

although there is something to be said for following the same pattern throughout in a method such as this. Not all links need to be indexed; some librarians might decide to ignore such entries as

Solos : Instrumental music.

It is only necessary to qualify each entry term by such terms in the chain as are essential to show the precise aspect of the subject :

Sonatas : Piano

not

Sonatas : Piano : Keyboard : Solos : Instrumental music.

However, it is important to remember that qualifying terms in an index entry, however many there may be, are always arranged in reverse order to the chain sequence.

Thus the chain reads

Piano
    Sonatas

therefore the index must be

Sonatas : Piano

not

Piano Sonatas.

The simplicity of the method is only fully realised if this basic rule is observed. It also reduces the number of entries which have to be made, thereby making it both an economic and a systematic method. In using the method in a general library, of course, the final qualifying term ' music ' would have to be added. In a special department it can be taken for granted.

DICTIONARY CATALOGUE

This type of catalogue is most widely used in America. It has very few adherents on the Continent but quite a number in Great Britain. For its successful use it is necessary to compile the subject headings from one of the published lists or to employ one of the mechanical methods such as chain indexing for doing this.

The dictionary catalogue is arranged in one alphabetical sequence, which includes entries for composers, authors, titles and subject, although in recent years the Americans have developed the divided dictionary catalogue, in which the different kinds of entry are arranged in separate alphabetical sequences. This fact alone is evidence of the difficulty of alphabetical arrangement. Further evidence can be obtained by comparing the Library of Congress *Catalog* 'Music and phonorecords', which is a composer catalogue with subject index, with the *British catalogue of music*. The *Music catalogue* of Liverpool Public Libraries, which to some extent avoids many of the difficulties inherent in the dictionary catalogue by not using specific entries, is further proof of the problems to be met in this kind of catalogue when it is used in a large library. In fact it is seen at its best in a catalogue to a fairly small collection and can possibly be recommended here in preference to the classified catalogue.

The basis of the syndetic dictionary catalogue as far as subject entries are concerned is that each item is entered under the most specific subject head that will contain it; or, to put it another way, the subject heading is coextensive with the subject of the book. The selected heading is then linked with related headings by a system of references. These references should ideally be made in all directions, but are generally only made from more general subjects to the specific subjects which they contain for reasons of economy. Sometimes references are made from co-ordinate subjects, that is, equally specific subjects:

Symphonies *See also* Sonatas

where it is felt that readers are likely to be interested in both. References are also made from synonyms which are not used as subject headings:

Folk music *See* Folk songs.

Probably the most generally used method of organizing such a subject catalogue is to base it on one of the published lists of subject headings. For a special library, the two general *Lists* issued in America (Sears and the Library of Congress) will not be detailed enough. Such libraries will find the *Music subject headings authorized for use in the catalogs of the Music Division* [of New York Public Library] useful. A foreword to the list explains the use of the headings provided.

This is a list which has developed to its present somewhat complicated form over a long period of time in a large public library. An examination of one or two of the terms will give some indication of its structure. For convenience, references are shown in square brackets, although they are not so shown in the list.

Oboe [*s.a.* English horn, Shawm, etc. *See* Flute for
    headings]
Oboe—Bibl. *See* OBOE MUSIC—BIBL.
Oboe—Instruction
Oboe music—Bibl.
Oboe—Orchestra studies [x Orchestra—Studies]
Oboe and Bassoon [xx Bassoon and Oboe]
Oboe, Clarinet and string orchestra [xx Clarinet, Oboe
    and string orchestra]
Oboe, flute, trumpet and string orchestra
See FLUTE, OBOE, TRUMPET AND STRING ORCHESTRA
Oboe in trios (oboe, bassoon, piano)
See PIANO IN TRIOS (PIANO, OBOE, BASSOON)
This continues to cover all possible combinations up to
Oboe in decets.
Sonata [xx Sonata da camera, Sonata da chiesa
    x Chamber music]
    criticism or analyses of sonatas by individual composers do
    not take this heading.
    Duplicate under instrument involved; e.g. a work on the piano
    sonata has subject 2—
    Piano—Music

It is difficult to see why the heading ' Piano sonatas ' is not used here. In fact this heading is not given at all. For some unspecified reason this list uses x for *See also* references and xx for *See* references, the reverse of the generally accepted way. These two examples do reveal the problems which the cataloguer faces in compiling subject headings. Frequently two entries have to be made if the item is to be satisfactorily entered, as in the case of instrumental forms such as piano sonatas. In addition, a very complex structure of subdivisions soon develops under one subject heading such as oboe. This is not easy to arrange alphabetically, and consequently the reader may well be confused. The Music Division of New York Public Library is justly famous for its service, and therefore any librarian using this list for his own library knows that it is based on good experience. If he is convinced that the dictionary catalogue is the better of the two traditional forms, he will find this list a good basis on which to work.

The aim of the New York list is to try to meet all likely approaches. Therefore, as it is a dictionary catalogue, there is entry of a composer's works under his name, while additional entries are provided by the list under instrument for the person interested in playing and under form for the scholar. Thus for a suite for clarinet two headings are provided:

Suites (Clarinet)

Clarinet music.

Such detailed treatment bulks the catalogue and some librarians may prefer to use the simpler list which can be built up from the *Music catalogue* published by Liverpool Public Libraries. Entries are made under the composer and the instrument, which is sub-divided into technique, solo, instrument and piano, duos etc. An exception is made for symphonies, but in the case of a composer like Haydn the reader is simply referred to the entry under the composer. The complicated treatment for ensembles in the New York list can be contrasted with the method used at Liverpool where such scores are brought together under 'Chamber music', sub-arranged by size and then by instruments. The American has the advantage of bringing everything relating to one instrument together under its name. In the Liverpool catalogue, entries under forms are limited to books about the particular form. References are very restricted, but the catalogue is easy to use and does add point to the criticism that references often confuse rather than help the reader.

CO-ORDINATE INDEXING

So many different methods have been given this name that it is perhaps invidious to select one and describe it under the general heading of co-ordinate indexing. Nevertheless in dealing with a small collection this system can be used to answer a wide variety of questions very effectively.

As each item is received it is given a number in succession. A card is made out for each term covered in the item and the number of the item recorded on each card. Thus after a number of documents have been received there will be a collection of cards, each bearing the name of a focus in music and the numbers of the items in which it is included. Therefore anyone interested in sonatas has only to turn to the relevant card and there find the scores, the numbers of which are recorded on the card. If Mozart's piano sonatas are required, then the cards for 'Mozart', 'piano' and 'sonatas' must be collated. The numbers common to all three cards will reveal the relevant scores. A sample check of such a system might show this:

Scores:

  1 Mozart's piano sonata no 1

  2 Beethoven piano concerto no 3

3   Brahms's clarinet sonata no 1
4   Hindemith's clarinet concerto
5   Mozart's piano concerto no 21.

Cards:

Mozart 1. 5.	Clarinet 3. 4
Piano 1. 2.3.5.	Beethoven 2
Sonata 1. 3.	Brahms 3
Concerto 2. 4. 5.	Hindemith 4

To use this sample to find a clarinet sonata, the cards reveal scores 3 and 4 for clarinet and 1 and 3 for sonata. The relevant score would be no 3—Brahms's clarinet sonata. A search for Mozart's piano music would reveal scores 1 and 5 to be applicable. Limit this to concertos and only no 5 is suitable.

The main disadvantage to this method is that the scores themselves cannot be arranged in any helpful order without some complication to the numbering, such as using the first three letters of the composer's name before each number to enable the scores to be arranged by composer. Thus the Mozart scores would be numbered successively as added MOZ 1, MOZ 2 etc. It also presupposes use of the catalogue for all searches, and obviously when the collection is large the whole method becomes too complicated. Nevertheless it is simple to compile and it does reveal a lot of information quickly. It could be used very effectively for a small collection of material where it is not convenient for the reader to handle the scores. It is obviously very suitable for a closed-access gramophone library.

The two traditional methods of arranging catalogues discussed here are practised widely by British librarians. The closer the examination of the dictionary and classified catalogues, the more evident do the advantages of the latter become. There seems to be no real reason why the classified file in the catalogue must be in the same order as the books on the shelves; therefore, even libraries which do not wish to change the shelf classification might find it advantageous to compile a classified catalogue using BCM and chain indexing. This provides a simple and economic method of giving the reader the maximum amount of information.

Co-ordinate indexing is closely linked to mechanical retrieval of information, a subject beyond the scope of this book but one which must engage the attention of music librarians as the demands on their services grow and the problems of arrangement and cataloguing increase.

Reference has already been made to the practice of some learned libraries, particularly on the Continent, of arranging their music according to one of the systematic arrangements devised by such scholars as Altmann and Hofmeister for their bibliographies. These would prove equally useful for a systematic catalogue, as is suggested in the international *Code* (page 47). It is interesting to note that this code suggests making as many entries for a work as are necessary to provide for all approaches. The scheme is very simple and would serve admirably for a small library, although the compilers suggest that only the main heads should be used in a small library.

Another approach suggested by the international *Code* is the alphabetical subject catalogue, this being kept quite separate from the composer catalogue. The suggestion here relates to the scores, and at its simplest this catalogue would consist of an alphabetical sequence of entries for works arranged by forms (sonata etc) or types (oratorio etc) or instruments (violin, voice etc). The more complicated sequence would be a combination of entries arranged by all kinds of heading. Obviously a lot would depend on the kind of information readers require in a particular library. It would be possible to provide all three kinds of heading, arranged in three separate sequences. Whatever the method adopted such a catalogue presupposes a separate title catalogue. An example of such a catalogue in use would be:

Mozart's piano concerto, к456.
Entries for this work under
  Piano (Instrument catalogue)
  Concerto (Form catalogue)
  Orchestra (Type catalogue).
Using all three kinds of entry in one sequence or in separate orders, this work could be traced under ' piano ', ' concerto ' or ' orchestra '. If readers were only interested in the instrument approach, then just the entry under ' piano ' would be used, possibly subdivided by concerto.

CHAPTER SIX

Arranging and cataloguing gramophone records

THE MAJORITY OF GRAMOPHONE LIBRARIES in this country are still closed access. This rather contradictory term applies to any library where the reader is not allowed direct access to the material he wishes to borrow, even when the pictorial sleeves supplied by the commercial record companies are displayed in browser boxes. The simplest method of arrangement for the records is by the record companies' catalogue numbers. These numbers are used throughout the trade, in all record reviews and in discographies; it follows that the reader who borrows records will be familiar with them as a means of reference, as he is more than likely to buy records as well. He will know the difference in quality represented by LXT, DGM and ALP, all of which are parts of catalogue numbers used by major companies, and it will not seem strange to him when he has to ask for a record by a number prefixed by such letters. In these circumstances there seems little point in a library adding its own accession number to be used as an arranging device.

Records in the BBC Gramophone Library are arranged first by the make and then by the catalogue number. This is a very simple system, but an equally simple method is to arrange directly by the catalogue number. Whichever of these systems is used, it will be more effective than one which is home made. It has the added advantage that the library's own catalogue can quite often be ignored. The reader can come direct from a search in a trade catalogue, discography or record review to the librarian. Whereas, if an accession number is used, he must first find this by consulting the library's catalogue.

There is, however, an increasing tendency for gramophone librarians to prefer open access, where the reader is allowed direct entry to the records, which will probably be housed in their sleeves in browser boxes. This is an excellent idea and it is unlikely to result in any serious damage to the records. The arrangement in the browser boxes need be only into broad groups such as 'symphonies', 'concertos', 'chamber music' and 'lieder'. It is important of course to separate the stereo from the mono records, when the former are provided, since they can be permanently damaged if played on mono equipment. In most libraries the turnover of records is very rapid, so there is little point in arranging by a detailed classification. Once again, as with the catalogue numbers, this arrangement by broad groups in browser boxes has the advantage of familiarity, as the reader will be used to the same method in record shops. Simple arrangement by composer can be used.

It would be possible to arrange records by the classification in use for scores and books, but this would not be easy as so many records are issued with more than one work, each quite often in a different form and by a different composer. As far as is known, only Liverpool Music Library has attempted to do this. Bliss made provision for such an idea in BC, however.

Records are not easy to consult when they are filed on ordinary shelves, as they would need to be if arranged by a close classification. The browser boxes make selection easier. In arranging by the broad classification, when a record includes two or three works one of these will have to be selected as the most likely to be sought. For records with more than three works it is probably best to have a group called 'collections' under instrumental and vocal.

A possible arrangement for browser boxes for display of classical records in sleeves, or the sleeves only when these are used as the indicator in a closed access system, might be:

MONO: *Instrumental*
    Collections
    Orchestral
    Symphonies
    Concertos
    Chamber music
    Sonatas and pieces for solo instruments.
Vocal
    Collections
    Sacred choral
    Secular choral
    Opera
    Songs

STEREO: A similar arrangement to that under mono, except that the division can be broader if fewer records are provided in this category.

Archive collections will almost certainly be closed access with only the staff allowed to handle the records. Here again arrangement by the trade catalogue numbers would seem to be the simplest method.

CATALOGUING

Most enquiries for gramophone records name the composer, but other common forms of request are for recordings of particular forms and instruments and by a named artist, orchestra or conductor. It is usual in gramophone libraries to arrange the main catalogue alphabetically by composer and to provide subsidiary alphabetical catalogues of artists, orchestras and conductors.

The only published codes for cataloguing records are the code for cataloguing music and phonorecords, that is the American *Code* discussed in chapter four, and *A manual for the cataloging of recordings in public libraries* by Dell DuBose Scholz issued by the Louisiana State Library in 1964.

The latter is intended as a simpler version of the American *Code*. Unfortunately the section of the international *Code* on gramophone records has not yet been published (December 1965) and a code of this kind has not been issued in this country. Very few libraries in Great Britain follow the American *Code* and therefore the following brief comment is based on general British practice, as far as such can be discovered. There would seem to be some agreement here with the methods suggested in the Louisiana State Library *Code*.

There are no particular problems in choice of form of composer's name and in designation of the work. British librarians tend not to use the American conventional title, but it seems to have as much to commend it for gramophone records as for scores. The title given to the work on the sleeve will frequently be different from that given on the label. Where this occurs, it is surely wiser to use the label title, as this will remain permanently with the record. In the heading for the composer entry the simple form of name (Bach, Beethoven, etc) is recommended as sufficient for all general purposes of identification as with scores.

When two or three works are recorded on one record, each should be entered separately. If a disc has works by several different composers with a collective title, some libraries enter it under this title with analytical entries under each composer, while other libraries prefer to enter each item separately. Discs with several works without a collective title can be entered under the composer of the first work on side one, or once again each work can be entered separately.

In the imprint and the collation, some libraries give rather elaborate details. The Louisiana *Code* calls for great simplification here and it certainly seems desirable. There is little point in giving the place of issue unless the record is foreign. The name of the particular label is more useful than the name of the company (Columbia rather than EMI). The date is useful and the date of release, not of recording, will be found on most recordings issued since the UK *Copyright act* of 1956 came into force. Some libraries give the trade catalogue number here, but if it is used by the library as accession number and filing medium for the record itself, it will be more useful at the head of the entry. The matrix number is quite unimportant for modern recordings and it could be described as pedantic to give it in a library catalogue.

If all the recordings in a library's collection are mono, 12 inch and 33⅓ rpm there is no point in stating this on every entry. If the majority are in this category only variations need to be entered. Some libraries indicate stereo/mono in the collation. Possibly the better way is to use a different coloured card for stereo records or to use an asterisk against the number which will itself indicate stereo (SXL is the Decca stereo sequence to their mono LXT). It is usual to indicate the number of sides a work occupies, but this can be omitted when the whole record is devoted to one work.

Two notes are usually given in a catalogue entry for a gramophone record. The first is a list of the performers, while the second is the *with* note which lists the couplings or companion pieces on the record. If conventional titles are used in the catalogue, the *with* note must list the couplings by the conventional and not the label title.

A typical entry might therefore be:

    Sibelius   *SBRG72351
       Concerto, violin, op. 47, D minor.
       CBS, 1965 (1 side).
    Zino Francescatti, violin; New York Philharmonic
    Orchestra; Leonard Bernstein, Conductor.
       With: Walton.   Concerto, violin, B minor.

For purposes of comparison a full entry for the Walton concerto is given, catalogued in accordance with the American *Code*:

    Walton, William, 1902—
       [Concerto, violin, B minor] *Phonodisc.*

70

Concerto for violin and orchestra. CBS, SBRG 72351, 1965.
1s.   12in.   33⅓ rpm.
Zino Francescatti, violin; New York Philharmonic
Orchestra; Leonard Bernstein, conductor.
With: Sibelius, Jean. Concerto, violin, op. 47, D minor.

The entries under names of artists are best filed in a separate sequence and should be as brief as possible, merely serving to guide the reader to the composer, title and catalogue number:
Francescatti, Zino, *violin.*   *SBRG72351.
Walton.   Concerto, violin, B minor.

Some libraries use larger cards than 5 in × 3 in for artists, and make entries on one card for several works as they are added to stock. This is certainly a great saving in space; otherwise, with entries for composers and all performers, the catalogue can become very large. Another space saving device is simply to refer from conductors to the orchestras with which they have been recorded. This involves the reader in a double search of course, but he will possibly be familiar with this method in *The gramophone quarterly catalogue.*

An alternative to the card catalogue is the visible index, where only the bottom edge of each card, bearing the brief identification of the work, is visible. This is used by some libraries as a combined catalogue and indicator. When a recording is available, a small disc is inserted into the perspex protecting the visible part of the card. If the reader wishes to borrow the recording he removes the disc and takes it to the librarian. The fuller details of the particular work are entered on the body of the card which can be revealed by flicking back the rest of the cards above it in the tray, each card being hinged into the tray to enable this to be done.

JAZZ AND FOLK MUSIC
Many libraries now stock these categories of music, which present very different problems in cataloguing from those found in handling classical recordings. To provide full information it would be necessary to enter under each title included on the particular record as well as under each artist, as enthusiasts in these two kinds of music are liable to search under either title or artist. Record companies are concerned only with selling the record and therefore are likely to use either of these items as a heading for it. The Louisiana *Code* suggests entering folk song albums under the unifying agent such as performer, title, arranger. This seems to be a very acceptable solution and would result in such headings for folk and jazz albums as:

Irish folk night
Fitzgerald, Ella
Newport Jazz Festival
Goodman, Benny, Quartet.

Where there are two unifying elements (Johnny Hodges and Duke Ellington) double entry would be necessary. If desired, brief references could be made from the names of artists and songs to the unifying elements chosen for the particular albums on which they appear. This solution may not be ideal in terms of theoretical cataloguing, but it does seem practical and once again is based on a familiar point of reference for the enthusiast.

SPOKEN WORD

Music librarians have been given the responsibility of organizing gramophone libraries, because the majority of recordings are still of music. However, there are now in existence a great many recordings associated with subjects such as railways, racing cars and childbirth, apart from the many of plays, poems and novels. The logical arrangement would be to place these in browser boxes in the appropriate section of the library, but until this is done, music librarians in charge of gramophone libraries will be faced with the problem of cataloguing such items. Plays, novels and poems can be treated as if they were in book form and present no problem. It is probably better to have a separate catalogue for such recordings. Recordings associated with other subjects are probably best treated in much the same way as illustrations in an illustrations collection, by compiling a subject index to them. Entry would be under the most specific head with the record number given as a reference. Thus a record of bird songs would have index entries under each species recorded with the label number of the record against it.

TAPES

Very few libraries stock pre-recorded tapes, which can be catalogued much as gramophone records. However, many libraries are now making their own recordings of local events and keeping them as part of the archive collection. Such a collection of tapes will be carefully catalogued, probably under subject, in accordance with rules for the archive collection.

The need here is for a careful system of reference to the particular point in a tape where any recording begins. The manufacturers of tape recorders have anticipated this by providing a counting device. Unfortunately these counters do not work to a standard pattern, but presumably the library will limit the playing of its tapes to its own machine and therefore this counter can be used as the point of reference in the catalogue entry. In addition it will be useful if each tape is given an accession number, which is shown in the catalogue as well as the speed at which the item was recorded.

This last is specially helpful where a four-track tape is used; identification of the track also helps.

CHAPTER SEVEN

Conclusion

THE EARLIER CHAPTERS have been concerned with the existing classification schemes and cataloguing codes and with the practice prevailing in some libraries. It is evident even from a very limited examination such as this that there is a very wide variety of methods which can be employed in organizing a music library. It is as well that there should be, for there are many different ways of approach to the art of music, and libraries must attempt to cater for all of them.

It is customary for the music librarian to have both knowledge of the subject and professional skill. Some even argue that the latter is unnecessary and that it is preferable to employ musicians as librarians. If there is a choice between a musician and a librarian without interest in music, it will probably be safer to choose the former, but it is not unreasonable to expect librarians to have both subject and professional knowledge, and there are many good music librarians who started their careers with the skills of librarianship and an enthusiasm for music, yet without a knowledge of its techniques, which they have acquired later. It is this love of their subject which will probably prevent music librarians of any kind from falling into the trap of becoming too concerned with the 'how' of their work and forgetting the 'why'.

The aim in organizing any material must always be simplicity, so that if possible the reader remains unaware of *how* he has been helped to find what he wants. With this in mind, many music librarians break away from a classified subject arrangement on their shelves in arranging scores while using a classification for the literature. Instead, they prefer to classify by physical format.

74

Thus there will be separate sequences of vocal scores, full scores, bound instrumental scores and miniature scores. Some libraries, such as the Central Music Library, arrange much of their instrumental music according to the instrument, unbound in pamphlet boxes. Such an arrangement might offend the keen librarian who likes everything neatly ordered, but it is very practical, easy to use and familiar to the reader, who will almost certainly have met the same method in music shops. Bound instrumental scores arranged on the shelves are classified by instrument, but vocal, full and miniature scores are best arranged alphabetically by composer within each sequence.

County libraries and other libraries which loan choral, orchestral and chamber sets, seem to find the easiest classification to be by these broad groups, sub-arranged by composer. Here again pamphlet boxes are very convenient for storage.

These methods are simple because they recognize physical differences, which in this case are more important than subject differences, and because they suit the approach of most readers. They will work in any kind of music library. The enquiry is usually by composer and, in the case of libraries loaning sets, the material is only handled by the staff, so this system is practical.

As has been stated, the literature will be arranged by a subject classification. This different approach to the two types of material presents no problem, even with DC where, according to the scheme, scores and books are arranged together, as the classification can be used for the literature and not for the scores. Some libraries have a curious practice of classifying the scores even when they are arranged alphabetically by composer.

In selecting the scheme to be used, choice should be based, as shown in chapter one, on an analysis of four factors—time, money, people and material. For complete coverage it would be difficult to better the BCM scheme, while a modification along the lines suggested by Maurice B Line (*see* bibliography) will be found very suitable for scholarly libraries. For simplicity, the McColvin scheme is recommended.

The information which the classification and arrangement on the shelves cannot supply will be provided by the catalogue. What form this takes will depend on the whim of the individual librarian. The most systematic method is the use of BCM with chain indexing. It has already been suggested that this method can be used in the catalogue, even where a different scheme is used on the shelves, but most librarians will probably prefer to use the same scheme on the shelves and in the catalogue.

There is much to commend the method whereby a number of

separate catalogues are provided for instruments, forms, composers and any other information generally required. The full entry is made under composers with a reference card in each of the other catalogues or indexes. The entries under each focus can either be arranged alphabetically by composer or chronologically by date of composition. Thus, using the latter method, an edition of C P E Bach's sonatas for flute and continuo would have a main entry in the composer catalogue, then the following possible additional entries in these supplementary indexes:

Index	Heading
Chronological	1740c.
National	German 1740*c*
Instruments	Flute 1740*c*
Forms	Continuo 1740*c*
	Sonatas 1740*c*

Very few libraries file entries for recordings with those for books and scores, but such a method would give complete coverage under each entry. The disadvantage probably lies in the bulk which such a combination catalogue would eventually have.

Music libraries collect other items besides books, scores and records. These include periodicals, programmes, concert announcements and useful items of information such as lists of piano tuners, teachers etc. With these, simple indexes are the best solution as they can the more easily be kept up to date. *Brio,* the official journal of the United Kingdom Branch of the IAML, now indexes articles on music in British periodicals. The index to concert programmes and announcements will probably need entries under composer, artist, title sometimes and possibly the writer of the programme notes. This index should be compiled on the same rules as those used in the general music catalogue and should not be attempted unless it can be kept up to date. The programmes are best arranged either chronologically or by concert hall.

Bibliography

THIS IS NOT INTENDED to be complete, but to list the items discussed and offer suggestions for further reading.

Classification—general:

Needham, C D *Organizing knowledge in libraries* Deutsch, 1964.

Palmer, B I and Wells, A J *Fundamentals of library classification* Allen & Unwin, 1957.

Music librarianship—general:

Bryant, E T *Music librarianship* Clarke, 1959.

Dove, Jack *Music libraries*. Original edition by Lionel Roy McColvin and Harold Reeves. Deutsch, two volumes, 1965.

Chapter one:

Farish, Margaret K *String music in print* Bowker, 1965.

Chapter two:

Coates, E J (*compiler*) *The British catalogue of music classification* BNB, 1960.

Coates, E J ' The British catalogue of music classification ' *in Music libraries and instruments: papers read at the Joint Congress, 1959, of the International Association of Music Libraries and the Galpin Society* Hinrichsen, 1961. Pages 156-165.

Line, Maurice B 'A classification for music on historical principles' *in Libri* 12 (4) 1962 352-363.

Chapter three:

Library of Congress *Classification: Class M, music and books on music* Washington, second edition, 1917.

Bliss, Henry Evelyn *A bibliographic classification* New York, H W Wilson, four volumes, 1953.

Dewey, Melvil *Decimal classification and relative index* New York, Forest Press, sixteenth and seventeenth editions (two volumes each), 1958 & 1965.

Ott, Alfons ' The role of music in public libraries of medium size ' *in Music libraries and instruments, op cit* pages 79-83.

Dove, Jack *op cit* pages 48-61.

BBC Music Library *Chamber music catalogue* BBC, 1965.

Four music bibliographies which are arranged systematically follow:

Altmann, Wilhelm *Kammermusik—Katalog* Leipzig Hofmeister, 1945.

Altmann, Wilhelm *Orchester—Literatur—Katalog* Leipzig, Leuckart, two volumes, 1926-36.

Becker, Carl Ferdinand *Systematisch—chronologische Darstellung der Musikalischen Literatur* Amsterdam, Knuf, 1964 (reprint of original 1836 edition).

Richter, Johannes F *Kammermusik—Katalog* Leipzig, Hofmeister, 1960.

Chapter four:

Music Library Association *Code for cataloguing music and phonorecords* Chicago, American Library Association, 1958.

International Association of Music Libraries *Code international de catalogage de la musique* Peters, 1957-. (Volume one: Grasberger, Franz *The author catalogue of published music* 1957; volume two: *Limited code* 1961.)

Chapter five:

New York Public Library *Music subject headings authorized for use in the catalogs of the Music Division* Boston, Hall, 1959.

Library of Congress. *Music and phonorecords* Washington, 1954-.

Liverpool Public Libraries *Catalogue of the music library* 1954.

Chapter six:

Scholz, Dell Dubose *A manual for the cataloguing of recordings in public libraries* Louisiana Library Association, 1964.

Currall, Henry F J (*editor*) *Gramophone record libraries* Crosby Lockwood, 1963. Pages 53-81 contain a full account of cataloguing practice at the BBC Gramophone Library.

Alvin, Mary, *and* Michelle, M 'La Roche College Classification system for phonorecords' *in Library resources and technical services* 9 (4) 1965 443-445.

Stiles, Helen J 'Phonograph record classification at the United States Air Force Academy Library' *in Library resources and technical services* 9 (4) 1965 446-448.

Index